HOW TO PLAN YOUR OWN HOME LANDSCAPE

HOW TO PLAN

YOUR OWN HOME LANDSCAPE

How to organize your outdoor space
and how to utilize it for maximum pleasure and
minimum maintenance all year round

by
NELVA M. WEBER
Photographs by
MOLLY ADAMS

Drawings by JOSEPH M. SAMMATARO

BOBBS-MERRILL   INDIANAPOLIS / NEW YORK

Portions of the book have appeared in periodicals;
my appreciation for permission to reprint from them
are extended to:

House Beautiful magazine for portions
of "How to Improve your Curves," October, 1975.

Massachusetts Horticultural Society
for portions of "How to Improve your Curves,"
Horticulture, June, 1972.

New York Botanic Garden for portions
of "Planting for Climate Control," *The Garden Journal,*
March-April, 1956.

New York Times Garden Page for portions
of "Make me no Landscapes," January 3, 1965.

The Small Homes Council-Building Research Council
at the University of Illinois kindly give
permission to redo six illustrations from Circular
C3.2, "Solar Orientation," for use in Chapter 3.

Designed by Philip Sykes
Manufactured in the United States of America

First printing

LIBRARY OF CONGRESS CATALOGING IN PUBLICATION DATA
Weber, Nelva M.
  How to plan your own home landscape.

  Includes index.
  1. Landscape architecture.   2. Landscape gardening.
  I. Adams, Molly.   II. Title.
SB473.W4   712'.6   75-33535
ISBN 0-672-51890-2

To Joseph   *counselor, co-worker, husband, friend*

ACKNOWLEDGEMENTS

Few of us truly walk alone. Many have helped to bring this volume to fruition, for which I am most grateful; unfortunately, it is not possible to list them all. Stanley White, design teacher par excellence, pointed the way. Fairy Godmother, Elizabeth Frost, was responsible for my first major commission. But it is to that great group of homeowners who had faith in my ability and who·were willing to execute my plans, that I am truly grateful. To them I owe the years of wonderful experience that made this book possible.

Landscape architects Edith Antognoli and Cornelia Sanders, and lifelong friend Helen Martini read and improved the manuscript. Thomas Smith Kelly helped with the chapter on lighting. Joseph M. Sammataro was a true collaborator in every sense of the word. Hanna Procidano and Carol Avallone patiently typed and retyped the manuscript. To them all, my thanks.

NELVA M. WEBER

To the many gracious ladies who so kindly let me wander through their "outdoor space" photographing the illustrations for this text, I am very grateful. I am particularly indebted to some of those belonging to the Somerset Hills Garden Club for their special interest.

And a special thanks to my husband, Urwin, for his good-natured tolerance of the many hours I spent traveling about, and working in the darkroom. As a photographer concerned with the visual, I am indeed happy there are people who care about the natural beauty around us, and about the art of landscape design.

MOLLY ADAMS

CONTENTS

INTRODUCTION:

ONCE
OVER LIGHTLY

Many people are interested in plants, both as living, growing things and as objects of beauty. Because they surround us in abundance there is a tendency to think of plants *as* the landscape. This is an error, however, for many interrelated elements make up the natural landscape: the land, mostly of rock overlaid with soil; the water; the atmosphere; and the sun, source of all energy. These basic units support a myriad of forms ranging from microscopic one-celled plants to giant redwoods. Without plants, life on earth as we know it would be impossible for they are the ultimate source of food and oxygen. Plants, in turn, could not survive without the animal world since they are dependent upon microbes, insects, birds, animals: the carbon dioxide producers, the pollinators, the decomposers. Thus the ongoing cycle of life is a working partnership between plant and animal life.

Due to this interest in plants themselves, people in general do not always distinguish between *planting* and *planning.* These two separate operations are often lumped together under that ambiguous and overworked term "landscaping." It may seem presumptuous to insist that landscape design is an art form and not a horticultural field, but such is the case. It is important for the layman to distinguish between the fine art of landscape *architecture* and a craft such as landscape *gardening,* or "landscaping," for the objectives and techniques characteristic of a fine art differ from those of a craft: art strives for the creation of beauty through arrangement, composition and design; a craft is involved in the construction or implementation of the component parts of a design.

Landscape design makes use of the same principles which are inherent in all good art: simplicity, good scale, balance, sequence and focalization. These principles are the guidelines in designing each outdoor feature—a flower garden, a shrub border, or a pool—but they also apply to the complete landscape design which represents the logical, unified arrangement of the individual elements comprising the whole. A good design should be simple—there should be no cluttered, or extraneous items, no unnecessary frills. Each part should be in good scale or proportion to the property: the parking area will be related to the family needs; the terrace will be in scale with the house and the demands placed upon it, as will the lawn and garden areas. There will be a balanced feeling in the spaces; this applies to outside "floor spaces" as well as to heights of buildings, trees and enclosures. Open spaces— lawns, terrace, ground cover areas and low shrub plantings—will be balanced against covered spaces such as buildings, arbors and canopy trees. These space relationships are most satisfactory if there is more open space than heavily planted or enclosed space.

The best landscape designs are never static; life and movement are needed to enliven the scene. The changing hours of daylight with its shifting shadow patterns, the mood of the winds from gentle breeze to violent storms, and the varied aspect of clouds and sky—these are nature's contribution. Nature is full of rhythm, of patterns repeated in varying cadence, and these elements too play a lively part in landscape design. Sequence is the eye traveling along a beautifully curving line or moving from one specimen to the next as it progresses down the garden border.

Last is focalization, a pause in the journey, a chance to examine and enjoy some feature of interest—a splash of water in the sunlight as it falls into a small pool, Saint Francis under a shadbush offering food to his feathered friends, a shady bower at the end of a brick path inviting the stroller to rest in its cool recess.

Plants are used to attain privacy and to enclose outdoor spaces; they give contrast between the open sunny spots and the secluded shady ones. They provide cover overhead and their shadows add interest and detail. Plants modify the abrasive elements of the climate and play a part in noise and pollution control. Not the least in importance, plants add social and spiritual amenities available in no other way.

This is not a book about planting, which is the final step in the development of any landscape. Instead it deals with that vital first step: planning, or the organization of outdoor space for use and enjoyment.

Part I is concerned with the family, the house and the land in terms of space for indoor-outdoor living. It stresses pre-planning—the importance of analyzing the needs and desires of the family, and the wisdom of trying optimum solutions in advance of actual execution.

Part II gives guidelines and presents various solutions applicable to the design and layout of outdoor spaces: an attractive and workable public space for entering and parking, a small but efficient service space and, most important, private outdoor space associated with the good life—terraces, lawns, gardens, recreation areas and enclosures with privacy.

Part III deals with practical improvements and refinements which add comfort, economy and safety to the landscape plan.

I
UNDERSTANDING THE LANDSCAPE

1

AMERICA'S MAJOR NATURAL LANDSCAPES

Planet Earth is a whirling sphere of rock, soil and water enveloped in a veil of atmosphere and warmed by radiant energy from a distant star. Every garden is a tiny segment of this larger landscape from which it receives a rich inheritance.

Some general understanding of natural landscapes adds greatly to the layman's enjoyment. For those interested in developing the land, the subject takes on far greater importance. By studying the great natural forms, by becoming familiar with their character and spirit, we, perhaps, can bring to our own small garden some of the inspiration we find in nature. The Oriental mind has long understood the importance of nature as the primary tutor. The designer must see and feel the landscape before he can really create fine garden art.

America is blessed with scenery of wide diversity: starting from the sandy beaches of the Eastern seaboard and the rock-bound coast of Maine, through the ancient worn-down mountains of New England and the scenic Appalachians, out across the broad expanse of prairie plains interspersed with breathtaking valleys and mysterious deserts, one comes at last to the rounded tawny hills of the California coast and the vast green forests and snowy peaks of the Pacific Northwest. The richness of form, color and texture and the enormous differences of scale are staggering to behold. There are endless variations but also repeated similarities, and these have been organized into a logical picture of the earth's features known as geomorphology, the study of landscapes. This not only enhances the appreciation of our scenic heritage, but can also contribute to the wise development of our own private garden.

Every landscape is the result of geologic phenomena, processes or agencies operating in accordance with age-old natural laws. Our continent is made up of two units, mountains and plains, bounded by an irregular coastline. Plains are the relatively level areas with horizontal layers of rock beneath the surface. Millions of years ago these plains lay beneath the sea. By means of mighty upheavals within the earth, they were lifted, intact, from the sea floor to become land. Mountains, on the other hand, came into being when the underlying rocks were deformed. Sometimes they were bowed up or corrugated or broken into huge blocks because of pressures within the earth. Sometimes molten rock poured forth to form volcanos.

These newly constructed plains and mountains were of gigantic size but they could not compare with the scenery of our present day world. It took millions of years of destructive forces at work—mostly wind and water—to carve and mold the details, to embellish and ornament the simple masses, to give charm and diversity to our present landscape. Streams carved out valleys, gorges, canyons, leaving peaks and ridges, depositing deltas and flood plains. Glaciers, grinding and gouging across mountains and plains, left cirques, moraines and drumlines in their wake. Waves cut sea caves, left cliffs and headlands standing, built up beaches and sand bars. Winds shaped mushroom rocks and piled sand into dunes. Ours is a sculptured landscape, especially in the West where the land forms are not softened with vegetation and the stark and jagged contrasts are most apparent.

The forces of construction and destruction continue to operate, slowly but surely, on our modern landscape; the earth is a battleground between two giants: one pushes up the land, while the other tears it down and dumps it into the sea. Constructive forces create the land but destructive forces provide the scenery.

One of the basic characteristics of any landscape is the visible topography growing out of the land's structural frame-work—its bones, as it were. The kind of bedrock and the various geologic processes that have fashioned it contribute to the form we see. A landscape of gently rolling hills evokes quite a different response from that produced by a majestic mountain range; so it may be said that landscape has spirit as well as form.

Some hills are individuals, rising above their surroundings, yet still part of the larger pattern. A feeling of comfort and serenity seems to accompany rounded hills. Mountains, with their barren rock and towering pinnacles, are dramatic compositions of strong vertical and diagonal lines, focusing at the top. However, each viewer interprets the spirit of the landscape differently. A jagged towering alpine peak may be an exciting challenge to a mountain climber, yet appear savage and even frightening to others.

The sea, the mountains, the plains and the forest—these are the big overpowering landscapes on which man makes but minor changes. We accept their dominating spirit, but we choose, develop and frame certain pictures within the whole. We may provide a foreground or screen out a disturbing portion. Near at hand are the smaller, more intimate land-scapes: the hills and the valleys, streams and ponds, beaches and sand dunes, rocky ledges and boulder-strewn fields. These smaller landscapes are more easily controlled and adapted; some portions may even be re-constructed or reproduced. One may yearn for a dramatic mountain pano-rama, yet enjoy a tiny backyard view that imparts its own quiet mood.

The true development of any home site begins with a feeling of respect for the land itself. The natural features of the land—the soil, trees, wildflowers, streams, swamps, rocky outcrops, birds and animals —have a value not always reckoned in determining the sales price for a plot of undeveloped land. These natural assets, so often eradicated by the bulldozers, can be evaluated on the basis of what it would cost to replace them. Indiscriminate bulldozing of sites could be stopped if developers were charged a destruction penalty equal to the appraised ecological loss. Penalities thus incurred would be paid to a public juris-dictional body to be used for buying and preserving wild areas of long-term environmental value—wetlands, flood plains, shorelines, streams, unusual plants and geologic features.

The late Aldo Leopold—forester, game manager and naturalist— first voiced a "land ethic" in his *Sand County Almanac,* published in 1948. He says: "We abuse the land, because we regard it as a com-modity belonging to us. When we see land as a community to which we belong, we may begin to use it with love and respect. . . . That land is a community is the basic concept of ecology, but that land is to be loved and respected is an extension of ethics. That land yields a cultural harvest is a fact long known, but latterly often forgotten."

Geologic features surround us on every hand. We need to see, recognize and understand them if we are to make wise use of our land. We may begin by "reading" our landscape, by delving into its geologic origin and ancient history. Is it part of an ancient mountain chain, the bed of an inland sea, a bit of recently emerged coastal plain? Its rocky origins have much to say regarding its form, soil, and plant cover. Inquire into its modern history. Has it been cultivated? Pastured? Is it woodland? Of what age? The answers give many clues that help us use the land wisely.

The United States is divided into several major landscapes known as physiographic provinces. Each comprises areas of similar origin and geologic history which thus share a basic form.

The Atlantic and Gulf coastal plains, chiefly layers of sand, clay and marl washed down off the highlands to the west and deposited in the ocean, were recently lifted above sea level by the earth's land-forming crustal movement. Most of the eastern coastline north of New York's Long Island have since been submerged and in this process the middle portion was also affected. River valleys were flooded and converted into the deep water ports of New York, Philadelphia, Baltimore and Washington, now surrounded by a highly industrialized area. The wide southern coastal plain with its mild climate and fertile lowlands became an agricultural area while the intervening sandy uplands supported pine woodlands. On its western rim the coastal plain abuts the Piedmont "oldland," low gently rolling hills which are the worn-down roots of ancient mountains composed of metamorphic rock. Rivers, flowing off the hard rocky land of the Piedmont onto the soft new land of the coastal plain, cut down rapidly, forming a series of waterfalls.

These became portage points which developed into Indian trading posts and eventually, fall-line cities of considerable importance.

The indigenous plants of the coastal plain coincide closely with the geologic boundaries, largely because of the new soils which tend to be dry, sterile and sandy. Such soils support several kinds of pine which continue to dominate as long as fires discourage the invasion of the oak forests. In wetter coastal areas of the south grow bald cypress, gum, ash and white cedar, often draped with Spanish moss. The peninsula of Florida, however, is a different and unique story. It is a recently up-arched underlying limestone bed, with many sink holes which became lakes or springs. From Miami southward, the plants of the coastal plain are replaced by the tropical flora of the West Indies. Coastal swamps are the home of salt-tolerant mangrove, while inland swamps such as the Everglades are covered with saw grass. Pines grow on the limestone ridges, and mounds or "hammocks" slightly higher than the low-lying flatlands are covered with dense forests and tangled vines.

All of the mountainous areas of eastern United States are known collectively as the Appalachian Highlands, with each division differing in age and composition. Easternmost are the complex metamorphic mountains of the New England Upland which face the Atlantic and extend southwest into New York, New Jersey and Pennsylvania. These are low but rugged mountains with an estimated age of over a billion years. A southern division—the low gently rolling Piedmont and the lofty Blue Ridge—extend into Georgia and Alabama.

To the west lie the Newer Appalachians, also known as the Ridge and Valley Province, stretching from Lake Champlain southwestward into Alabama. This is a mountain range of younger layered or sedimentary rocks which have been folded, arched up and broken, then uplifted and eroded to form parallel landscapes of charming agricultural valleys on the softer shales and limestones, alternating with forested ridges of more resistant rock. The river systems of the folded Appalachians exhibit a peculiar pattern known as trellis drainage, which looks something like a grape vine on an arbor; this is quite apparent on a road map and from the air.

The western portion of the Atlantic Highlands, known as the Appalachian Plateau, includes the Catskills of New York and the Cumberland Mountains to the south. Here the rock layers lie horizontally, since they escaped the violent folding process which formed the Newer Appalachians. It is a rugged landscape of high mountains separated by deep valleys cut by swiftly flowing streams. Here the rivers follow the usual "dendritic," or tree-like pattern.

Eastern United States is well watered the year round and the widely varied landscapes of the Atlantic Highlands are the home of the eastern deciduous forest which once covered hundreds of thousands of square miles. This is a forest of tall trees forming a closed cover overhead, with a well-spaced understory of shrubs. The forest floor displays a number of early blooming wildflowers, ferns and low, broad-leaved evergreens as well as shade-tolerant asters and goldenrod. The richest forests are found in the southern Appalachians; in other areas beech and sugar maple grow on the better soils with oak and hickory on the drier, more exposed locations. In New England, hemlock intermingles with beech and sugar maple; other areas were covered with stands of white pine. Remnants of this once extensive forest still clothe the highest, roughest portions of the land. Valleys and reasonably level land have been appropriated for agriculture or development and in many places the forest has been greatly modified.

The great central heartland of our country presents quite a different picture—a seemingly endless expanse of flat to gently undulating land beneath a great dome of sky. This is plains country. Beneath the black soil lie horizontal layers of rock laid down as sediments in the waters of inland seas which once covered the interior portions of the continent. Gently uplifted, it became land of low relief. Since our weather pattern travels from west to east, the moisture-laden clouds from the Pacific are "wrung dry" before they reach the plains, which is why the plains are grasslands. Grasses can survive with small amounts of moisture, for they lie dormant in winter but grow quickly again with the arrival of spring rains. The western plains are covered with short grasses which can survive on 10 to 15 inches of annual rainfall. The eastern prairie plains, where rainfall is more abundant, once supported tall grasses interspersed with myriads of wildflowers. Vast plains throughout the world were once, and in some places still are, inhabited by nomadic people with movable homes, and flocks or herds which foraged on the grasses. Our western plains are still grazing areas, but cattle and sheep have replaced the pronghorn and the buffalo. Moving eastward the grasses have yielded to cultivated crops of wheat; the tall grass prairie is now covered with fields of corn and soybeans.

The heartland has changed its face, but not its spirit. Its broad expanses give a feeling of vastness and overwhelming simplicity like the ocean, yet without a sense of impending danger—it is an effect produced by no other land form. There is a certain monotony about it, but when one stands on that flat surface with the sky arching all around—with a glorious, unimpeded view of sunsets and stars—one feels directly in touch with the great natural forces of the world.

The western third of the United States is a region of mountains and plateaus. Traveling westward across the plains, the approaching mountains may appear like a low-lying cloud bank on the horizon. On a clear day from a distance of a hundred miles the Rockies may rise abruptly from the plains and, as the miles spin by, a breathtaking panorama unfolds. Compared to the ancient worn-down Appalachians, the Rockies are young, with high jagged peaks and steep rocky slopes. While they were formed a mere 60 million years ago, their bones are of ancient crystalline rock, perhaps a billion years of age, with a covering of younger layered rock that was once deposited in an ancient sea. In an era of mountain building, land was pushed up to great heights; the layers of overlying sedimentary rocks were broken and eroded into parallel ridges called "hogbacks," exposing the ancient core which we

1. *These fields were once an ocean floor.*

2. *Contemporary man all too often sees the land merely as property. It is his to develop or abuse—so he scars its face with earth-shattering machinery, and pollutes and poisons its soil and water.*

now see in the high peaks and uplands of the Rocky Mountains.

Even more spectacular are the Northern Rockies. Not only have they been uplifted, folded and eroded, in some places great blocks of the earth's crust were faulted or broken and pushed up and over the surrounding surface. Striking examples of such overthrusts are found in Glacier National Park, where brightly colored bands of layered rock are found on mountain tops.

Most of the western mountains are covered with coniferous forests which are zoned according to elevation. As high altitudes and high latitudes often support similar plants and animals, in a single day one may travel along Trail Ridge Road from the plains to the Arctic merely by driving from Loveland, Colorado, to above timberline at Alpine Station in Rocky Mountain National Park. On this trip one would experience five life zones. From Loveland in the high plains, 4,000 to 6,000 feet in elevation, one enters the park in the foothills which range from 6,000 to 8,000 feet. Here the dry slopes are clothed with short grass and colorful wildflowers in open parklike stands of tall ponderosa pine. The Montane zone, 8,000 to 10,000 feet, has everything: a primeval forest of tall slender lodgepole pines, charming mountain parks or large open meadows, aspen groves in moist valleys, and dense forests of Douglas fir on the north slopes.

Next comes the subalpine, extending from 10,000 feet to timberline, with a thick dark forest of spruce and fir standing close for protection from the searing winds. Limber pine and bristle cone pine grow singly or in small groups and tolerate the windswept spots. Near timberline, evergreen trees grow as prostrate shrubs, then disappear entirely, leaving the mountain tops bare save for the low cushionlike clumps of wildflowers and lichens of the alpine tundra. In the Rockies timberline is approximately 11,500 feet.

The Rocky Mountains chain is separated from the far western mountains by two vast plateaus. To the south lies the Colorado Plateau, nearly 130,000 square miles, centered roughly at the point where

Colorado, Utah, Arizona and New Mexico meet. A land of horizontal structure and high elevation, it is essentially a young landscape with a flat skyline and a few swift rivers in deep canyons cutting through

3. This view of Bear Mountain Bridge shows how harmoniously technological forms can blend with the surrounding forms of nature.

4. *In garden design natural landscape forms are complemented by plant material. Here the dramatic vertical spire of a mullein pierces the horizontal bands of the distant mountains.*

successive layers of sedimentary rock. Nowhere is the horizontal character of the plateau more dramatically displayed than in the Grand Canyon of the Colorado River. Men once thought that great rifts in the earth's surface were caused by cataclysmic forces: the earth suddenly parted and a great canyon was born. But in this parched landscape, running water is the sculptor of this majestic scene. It has already cut through colorful layers of limestone, sandstone and shales some 6,000 feet in thickness and now flows on basement crystalline rock at least a billion years of age. From the canyon one sees a slice of the earth's crust much as an ant views the interior of a layer cake from which a wedge has been cut.

Elsewhere on the plateau water has washed away the softer shales and weaker sandstones, leaving cliffs, buttes and mesas capped with resistant rock such as those strange formations found in Monument Valley. Dramatic scenic attractions are abundant in this dry land: Bryce and Zion canyons, Mesa Verde and the Petrified Forest, to name a few. Geologically, they are the remnants of erosion.

The plateau may also be divided into life zones. The north rim of the Grand Canyon belongs to the Canadian zone, similar to the Montane zone of the Rockies. Here the high elevations bring ample rain and cool temperatures which support forests of Douglas fir, white fir, blue spruce and aspen. Below this lies the Transition zone corresponding to the foothills in the Rockies. It too has well-spaced ponderosa pines. The south rim of the Grand Canyon is semi-arid with a scrubby covering of juniper and pinyon pines; it is known as the Upper Sonoran life zone. A mile lower at the bottom of the canyon one experiences the tropical climate of Mexico.

The Columbia Plateau is a different kind of landscape, both in aspect and in history. This somber, brooding, often desolate land is of volcanic origin. Some fifty million years ago molten rock or lava poured forth from the earth's deep caldron and spread out over the surface in great floods, filling the valleys and surrounding the hills, building up layers to depths of thousands of feet. A canyon cut into the plateau by the Snake River has exposed twenty layers of lava, some as much as a hundred feet thick.

This volcanic landscape extends from the Grand Tetons of Wyoming west to the Cascades, covering more than 100,000 square miles of southern Idaho, eastern Oregon and southwestern Washington. Lava flows as recent as five hundred years ago look vaguely like the moonscape. Eventually even these unlikely spots will support sturdy pioneer plants. This is cool desert country in the rain shadow of the Cascades, and vast areas are clothed with sagebrush interspersed with bunch grasses; flowers appear with the spring rains. Seasonal grazing exists in some areas and fruit and wheat are grown where irrigation is possible.

South of the Columbia Plateau is the Great Basin, our largest desert, which includes most of Utah and Nevada and parts of adjoining states. Much of this vast basin has no drainage to the sea. In addition to Great Salt Lake, the remnant of ancient glacial Lake Bonneville, there are smaller salt lakes and barren alkaline playa. Plants of the lower elevations include sagebrush, greasewood and shadscale, giving a gray-green look to this endless expanse of space. Clumps of grass and scattered sego lilies, lupine and Indian paint brush add a bit of seasonal color. The narrow north-south mountain ranges of the basin are cooler and less arid and support low open desert forests of junipers, pinyon pine, scrub oak and mountain mahogany. The Columbia Plateau and the Great Basin are desert landscapes largely because they lie in the rain shadow of high mountains to the west. Moisture-laden west winds, cooled as they reach the high slopes of the Cascades and Sierras, drop heavy rains on western slopes but continue eastward across the desert as warm dry winds.

In northern California, Oregon and Washington the majestic peaks of the Cascade Range in their classic conical form reach upwards to more than 14,000 feet above sea level. Their lower flanks are swathed in dense coniferous forests of Douglas fir, western hemlock and red cedar with mountain hemlock and western white pine on the higher elevations. The meadows are blanketed with several hundred varieties of wildflowers. The Cascades are young mountains, a combination of recent lava flows and volcanic eruptions, born of tremendous disturbances within the earth. Crater Lake, a mountain jewel, lies in the collapsed bosom of a 12,000 foot volcano that has blown its top.

The Cascades come to an end with Mt. Lassen, and the Sierra Nevadas begin. Here is a different kind of geologic formation known as a block mountain. A great block of granite 400 miles in length was cracked along a fault or zone of weakness and lifted high in the air, its steep eastern face rising abruptly out of the desert and the long top side sloping gently westward to the central valley of California. Erosion by water and ice have transformed the Sierras into spectacular scenery. Yosemite, with its glacial valleys and tall wispy waterfalls, is a prime example.

The slopes of the Sierras are drier than the Cascades and the vegetation is similar to that found in the Rockies. Ponderosa pine on the lower slopes gives way to Jeffrey pine, red fir and sugar pine as the elevation increases. The middle altitudes are famous for the giant sequoia or "big tree" with a girth of 25 feet.

The Pacific is rimmed with a range of mountains which sweep down from Canada into the United States as the Olympic Mountains of Washington and continue as the Coastal Range of Oregon and California. From San Francisco northward the ocean provides the moisture and moderate temperatures that are ideal for forests. Some of the world's tallest and most magnificent trees are found in the Pacific Northwest: dense forests of Douglas fir, western red cedar, western hemlock and Sitka spruce. The fog belt of the Coast range in Oregon and northern California is the home of giant coastal redwoods.

Between the Coast range and the Cascade-Sierra complex lies a lowland trough which is an extension of the Inland Passage of the west coast of Canada. It continues southward as the Puget Sound, the Willamette Valley of Oregon, the great central valley of California, the Imperial Valley and is out to sea once more with the Gulf of California. Since the central valley of California lies in the rain shadow of the Coast range, it receives a limited amount of a rainfall and was originally grassland but is now extensively irrigated and cultivated.

Southern California differs from most of continental United States in that it has a Mediterranean type of climate—dry summers with rains only in the winter, which is of little use to trees. Here the plant cover is known as chaparral: shrubby thickets of small-leaved evergreens which sprout up quickly when burned over. At higher elevation in California, Arizona and New Mexico there are open woodlands of evergreen oaks.

The warm deserts of the Southwest are a continuation of the Great Basin and include southeastern California, and portions of Nevada, Arizona, New Mexico, Texas and northern Mexico. Here the rainfall may be less than 5 inches per year and the spare vegetation is especially adapted to cope with high temperatures and little moisture. The creosote bush regularly spaced 15 to 30 feet apart is found throughout the southwestern desert. Major divisions of the desert are known for their usual plants. The Mohave in southeastern California is famous for a yucca known as the Joshua tree. The saguaro cactus is found in the Sonoran Desert of Arizona, and the yellow-flowered agave known as lechugilla survives in the white gypsum sands of the Chihuahuan desert in New Mexico.

We are indeed fortunate in the wide diversity of our country. Each home plot inherits from this larger landscape its climate, soil, water, the plants and animals of its ecological communities, plus a certain individual personality which deserves understanding and respect. Yet wise use of the land does not depend totally upon size of plot or geographic location. A successful home landscape results from the planning of outdoor space which joins the family and the architecture in a cooperative venture with the land.

2

HOME IS MORE THAN HOUSE AND GARDEN

Once upon a time, tall well-cared-for houses looked out on elm-shaded Main Streets of many towns. Their front doors, opening onto porches with swings and rocking chairs, were the essence of hospitality. The back doors led to long narrow yards containing vegetable gardens, the ash heaps and stables. Large gracious homes still line some Main Streets, minus the elms, but life within is not the same, and most of them have been bulldozed to make way for smaller homes, shops and office buildings. The age of technology has altered our way of living, both indoors and out.

The high cost of land and construction, the lack of domestic help and gardeners, and the change of life style in an automated age have revolutionized home architecture and the backyard. For contemporary house design, geared to the 20th century, the architect takes the family as his focus and tries to solve its needs in terms of today's living. Thus we have the family room, the liveable modern kitchen, built-in storage and the attached garage. Houses have become smaller, lower, more spread out on the land; there are more doors and larger areas of glass (even if only a picture window or sliding glass doors), resulting in a closer relationship between interior and exterior. Today's houses spill into an outdoors geared for active work and play—eating, entertaining, relaxing and, of course, gardening. The old backyard has become a new landscape for people—a place to look out at and to live in.

The budget for a new home once included the lot, the house and the furniture, with a small amount saved for the outside. The lawn and planting was done after the house was built, largely as a cosmetic effort to conceal the scars inflicted by the building process. "Foundation planting" tied the house to the ground, softening its lines and sometimes helping to conceal architectural faults. The homeowner's enthusiasm for fast-growing and ultimately large-sized trees, shrubs and evergreens often resulted in gross overplanting.

In today's marriage of indoor-outdoor spaces, this limited beautification approach is out-moded. Those who buy land and build a new home may find it surprisingly complicated and expensive. The cost of the land plus the cost of site development—driveway, parking, walks, steps, fences, walls, drainage, irrigation, grading, outdoor lighting and additional structures—adds up to a sizeable investment. Furthermore, most site work must be done before the house is occupied, and may cost anything from a fifth to a third of the total investment. On difficult terrain it may amount to as much as the house itself.

Those who buy a "builder's house" may also have problems. In fast-growing areas where open land is being covered with row upon row of depressingly similar houses, the developer is seldom interested in the long-range view. A certain amount of site work is sometimes required by local zoning regulations but there may be few controls. Too often problems are simply passed on to the buyer to become a millstone around his neck. Many of them involve surface drainage or water-logged soils which should never be used for building sites. Swamps and wetlands serve a vital role in our ground water supply and should be preserved as natural reservoirs.

Here and there one finds a far-sighted individual who spends many hours in pre-planning for that happy day when house and land will combine in a satisfying arrangement of indoor and outdoor space designed for living, work and play, with due consideration for privacy, convenience, pleasure and beauty. He undoubtedly begins by weighing the assets and the liabilities of the land itself. Is the soil fertile, rocky, sandy, swampy? Are slopes steep or gentle enough to be usable with little grading? Are there enough well-placed shade trees?

What of the house? Do living areas face south or northwest, the street or the back of the property? Does the house lend itself to indoor-outdoor living? Is it possible to achieve privacy? Is there a spot for outdoor sitting and entertaining, cool and shady in summer, sunny and protected from the winds of late fall and early spring? Is it convenient for serving food and drinks? What about storage space for tools, outdoor furniture and garden supplies?

What of the family's individual needs and interests? Is there a spot for a toddler's sandbox and bicycle, near at hand yet not underfoot? A place for teen-age activities—badminton, barbecues, moonlight music sessions? An herb garden near the kitchen for the cook; a small rose garden to satisfy a hobbyist? A bird corner for the family naturalist?

Does space permit off-street parking for a couple of cars? Will garbage and delivery trucks be able to turn around? Is the family entry convenient for the housewife, loaded down with the week's marketing? Are outdoor steps well-proportioned and easy to climb? And what about the tremendous problem of maintenance? Will the owner be a garden slave or master of all he surveys? Will he consider form and line, the relation of open space and enclosure, the silhouette of a shrub border, the delicate tracery of a summer shade tree, the subtle line of a path that delights the eye while leading to its destination?

Such questions have to do with analysing and defining the problems at hand and gathering data upon which to base intelligent planning. The land, the house and the family are a triple alliance, since each must serve the other, but the starting point must be the family— its size, the ages of its children, the parents' hobbies and patterns of entertaining, the lifestyle most congenial to the family as a whole. From this should follow the actual design of house and landscape and the subsequent operations of building, grading, paving and planting.

Design implies a space relationship. People live in space, their houses being enclosed or covered space with three dimensions—length, width and height. Outdoor or open space has the same three dimensions. It is easy to see the length and breadth of the land; less easy to comprehend the air space or volume so vital to landscape design. This can be visualized if we think of earth as the floor, shrubs as the walls, and the ceiling as a canopy of trees or a combination of trees and sky.

Our lives are filled with sensations of space, both exhilarating and terrifying; these impressions help to mold our lives for better or for worse. Since space is really a measure of the quality of human environment, attempts have been made to legislate minimum living space. Alas, size alone is not enough. The quality of space must be considered. Space is the frame within which the lawns and gardens of the home scene are sculpted.

Indoors and outdoors should be complementary, each making the most of the other. The design should use the land to best advantage,

5. *A particularly lovely and elegant example of the present day relationship between indoor and outdoor living.*

emphasizing its assets, subordinating its liabilities—a unique solution for a unique bit of earth. Next, the landscape design should be beautiful: a harmonious spatial experience from which the family derives satisfaction. Finally, it should be a solution which lies within the limitations of the site, and one which can be constructed and maintained within the budget and the capabilities of the owner.

6. *The old backyard has a new attractive look and a wonderful variety of uses. It's now a place to eat and entertain in—a place in which to relax, read a book, sunbathe, perhaps even take a swim.*

7. *The far-sighted owners of this home carefully planned this happy marriage of house and lot to give them exactly the features they wanted, could afford and easily maintain.*

8. *The plan includes a circular terrace serving both living room and library and a small fence-enclosed garden in two parts: an herb garden and a rose garden adjoining the tiny greenhouse. Two upright growing callery pear trees offer noonday and early afternoon shade; the house itself shades the terrace in the late afternoon.*

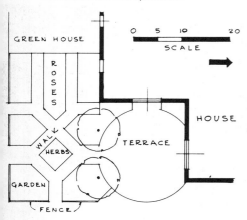

9. *All garden details are important. This honey locust tree gives shade to the terrace but in a charming way with delicate foliage and a soft shadow pattern.*

10. *Landscape design is the practical arrangement of trees, terraces, flowers, etcetera, for human use and enjoyment. It is a marriage of man and nature and art.*

3

PRE-PLANNING THE HOME SITE

Site planning is concerned with man's physical environment. Since he is indeed an animal not so long removed from wild nature, the earth, sun, air and water are of intimate importance to him. Primitive man had a relationship with environment which we have lost in the process of becoming civilized. Communal animal societies such as the wolf family still live in harmony with nature, using its resources without polluting or exhausting them. Only man fouls his nest and his planet.

The Oriental designer would contemplate the site, meditating on each stone, each tree, each undulation in the earth's surface. He noted the wind and the rain, the shadows and the highlights, the mood of each passing hour. He experienced the site to its fullest before attempting to design for it. Our modern life seldom permits meditation of any kind and very little goes into site planning.

"Site" refers to a parcel of land to be developed by the owner. It is his to use as he sees fit. Unfortunately, few owners realize that their small parcel of land can never be entirely divorced from the surrounding landscape. The surface of the earth is a continuous mantle of soil and rock; the ground water on any one site also underlies the land around it and the whole region shares the same sun and atmosphere. It is self-evident that anything done to a single piece of land affects the surrounding environment.

Many things that make for comfort, beauty and pleasant living are built into the land itself and it is important to recognize these qualities early enough to preserve them. In fact, the time to check assets and liabilities is *before* the land is purchased.

Climate is an integral part of every parcel of land. The sunlight varies with hourly and seasonal directions. The prevailing winds of summer and winter are inherent in the site, and so is elevation—actual elevation above sea level, and relative elevation, that is, the relation of the land to the surrounding areas. Each site has its own slope or gradient, varying in direction and steepness. All of these things have some bearing on the possibilities of the site.

Though we are often considered a nation of sun worshippers, it is surprising to find that many people have only a hazy idea of the sun's direction. The primitive bushman located his hut with great care; without the blessings of heating and air-conditioning, he used the natural forces to their greatest advantage. (Such expertise actually continued up to the 20th century and is now being reintroduced in solar-heated houses.) Historically, orientation to the sun or to the points of the compass has played a role in many civilizations, including the Aztec and the Greek, and in the siting of religious architecture. With the energy crisis upon us it behooves us to consider the directions of sun and wind relative to the house, which in turn affect indoor and outdoor light, shade, warmth and comfort. Careful orientation can reduce the load on heating and cooling systems and thus help to save on energy. It should also be considered in placing such outdoor features as parking areas, driveways, terraces, gardens and swimming pools.

Modern man as well as his primitive ancestor needs the sun to serve a variety of purposes: it warms his house in winter and saves on fuel bills; it melts snow and ice from drive and garage court; it dries up muddy soil and moisture-laden air. It makes trees, grass and garden grow. Even more important, it warms man's spirit and makes him feel better physically and psychologically.

To make use of this free energy, it is important to know something of the seasonal variations in the sun's pattern. Of major importance is the difference in angle of the noonday sun in winter and summer. The winter sun is relatively low in the southern sky, and its rays penetrate far into south-facing rooms if these are provided with adequate windows. Rooms facing north will receive no sun at all. The radiant heat of the sun, transmitted by infrared rays, passes through glass on a short wave-length. These strike and warm the floor, walls, ceiling and furnishings in the room; they are then re-radiated on a longer wave-length which cannot pass out through the glass. Though large south windows of Thermopane or other forms of double glazing cost more to purchase and install than average windows, they will almost always reduce the annual fuel bill. However, the size of the heating plant must be adequate to provide a comfortable indoor climate during sunless weather.

Winter sun is welcomed in our houses, but the hot summer sun is another story. Fortunately it shines down from a high angle so that only a relatively small amount enters the house. Even more important, the summer noonday sun can be excluded from the interior, without reducing the winter benefits, by means of horizontal projections over the windows. Carefully placed outdoor terraces and sun pockets which are bathed in winter sun can be protected from summer sun by properly located deciduous trees.

Not only does the sun's angle vary with the seasons, its hourly direction changes from month to month. Most people think of the sun as rising in the east and setting in the west. So it does, in mid-March and mid-September. In a wide east-west band across the United States the June sun appears in the northeast before 5 a. m. and sets in the northwest about 7:30 p. m. By contrast, the December sun rises in the southeast about 8 a. m. and sets in the southwest about 4 p. m.

What does this mean when translated into creature comfort? In winter only south-facing walls and windows are bathed in sunlight; in summer the hot sun hits east and west walls. In summer and winter, east exposures are more comfortable than west. The summer noonday sun is generally acceptable; the thermometer is still climbing, but the sun's rays strike the house walls at an acute angle. It is the afternoon sun which is uncomfortable to man and beast alike. Between 3 p. m. and 5 p. m. air temperatures peak, and the descending sun strikes the west walls head-on, transmitting a maximum of radiant heat. No amount of roof overhang can exclude these nearly horizontal rays in June and July.

Land with a desirable solar orientation should provide a house with a possible south, southeast or southwest exposure. For the maximum sun available in any one area choose a south-facing slope, for it receives more sun than comparable flat land. A site with the latitude of New York City, sloping toward the south at a 10 per cent gradient (1 foot of vertical drop in 10 feet horizontal distance), will receive as much direct radiation from the sun as flat land with a latitude equivalent to Memphis, Tennessee. This is because the rays of the sun hit the land at a more direct angle on a south-facing slope—spring comes earlier and autumn lingers; there are fewer record-breaking minimum winter temperatures. South slopes are hot in summer but no hotter than other areas, and north slopes are often just as hot—since the summer sun sets in the northwest, a north slope may receive as much as fourteen hours of sun while the south slope receives only seven or eight. Thus a house located on a southeast slope receives a maximum of winter sun, and a minimum of hot late-afternoon summer sun.

The directions of prevailing winds are also important. Wherever possible, good exposure to summer breezes and protection from cold winter winds should be sought. Local situations will bring variations, but in many parts of eastern United States, for example, summer breezes come from the south and west while winter winds come out of the north and northwest.

Much of our summer discomfort is caused by humid stagnant air. Moving air has a cooling effect. If living areas of the house face toward the prevailing summer breezes and if there are adequate doors, windows or vents to provide air circulation through the house, a type of natural air-conditioning operates.

Air circulation is influenced by the topography of the land. Summer breezes sweep open south or southwest slopes if unincumbered by dense plant cover. They can also be encouraged by clearing or cutting air lanes parallel to the prevailing winds through heavily planted areas.

North slopes receive an abundance of summer sun but may also be hot because of poor summer air circulation. In winter the situation may be reversed, with cold winds sweeping out of the north and northwest. Winds on the leeward side of a slope are usually quieter than those on the windward side, but if the windward side is steep and the leeward slope is gentle, the latter may be windier. A higher elevation to the north of a house site may help to protect it from adverse winds; a windbreak to the north and northwest can reduce the wind speed by one-half for a distance ten times the height of the windbreak. All slopes are modified by a cover of vegetation, for plants tend to produce a quieter, cooler, more humid and stable climate.

Changes in elevation bring changes in temperature, especially at night. Cold air gradually settles on the ground in flat areas. Where there are hills and valleys, the cooler air gradually flows downhill as if it were molasses, collecting in the low spots. On clear calm nights these low places become frost pockets while the slopes above may remain frost-free. In summer, valleys filled with cool air are often pockets of fog by morning and remain so until the sun burns it off or the wind dissipates it. In winter they may be cold pockets with temperatures lower than those on the surrounding hillsides.

Shore breezes from the ocean or a large lake blow from the water to the land by afternoon and from the land to the water by night. In choosing a house site by the shore, locations on the upper and middle slopes are to be preferred over those on the crest or the base of the slope.

A check list of assets for a good site may include: a southern exposure to provide winter sun; availability of summer breezes for cooling; protection from winter winds; sufficient elevation to provide good air drainage; a pleasant view if possible, combined with privacy, good deciduous shade trees, preferably south and west of the house, and an easy access to a quiet street. In ready-made neighborhoods one must assess shopping, transit, schools, churches, nuisance-type institutions, industries, noise pollution, and proximity of neighbors' houses and yards.

The ideal site development is a beautiful blend of land and architecture. Once the right land is found, the right house should be planned to complement it. In such a house the living space and the Thermopane areas should face south with perhaps a slight deviation toward the west. The east side, open to the morning sun, would have moderate amounts of glass, while the west would be shielded from the mid-afternoon sun by vines or trees. Every attempt should be made to orient the house so that it can bask in the winter sun and be spared the afternoon heat of summer. However, a house designed for a particular site may be less than perfect if built elsewhere. The same house plan should not be used on streets facing different directions if houses must be lined up parallel with the street, or if there is not sufficient space to locate each one advantageously.

Solar orientation along with privacy and a view may also be difficult to achieve for houses built on small lots facing north-south and east-west streets. Large windows should not look out on an unattractive or a limited view or be shaded by a house to the south. A translucent glass wall substituted for clear glass will let in light but afford privacy. In a house that faces both south and the street, average sized windows with normal sill heights will let in sun without turning the house into a goldfish bowl. The best choice on a small lot has the outdoor living space south of the house; here large windows flood the house with sunlight, privacy is possible and the garden can be an extension of the living room.

Important though comfort may be, it is not everything. Home-owners who feel that beauty is as basic as utility, should consider the natural features of the land. Decidous trees south and west of the house are decided assets. Good friable well-drained soil is basic. An area of open sunlit grass, combined with a wooded area, makes for varied and attractive results. Views are to be sought out and developed, though not at the expense of privacy. Any existing natural features should be used to advantage. A natural ledge of rock may be developed as an alpine garden, and a marshy spot may become a small pond if there is an adequate watershed. A high spot can be turned into a lookout or the site of a garden gazebo. A huge oak may determine the location of a terrace or even the house itself. These are aesthetic qualities that supplement the practical assets of the site. Ready-made designs are seldom transferrable to different sites. A successful plan evolves from the site itself, its existing vegetation and its natural forms and features. Size of plot is not important. The same principles of wise land use apply to small lots as well as large, to suburban as well as exurban places.

People have more innate outdoor knowledge than they realize, and need not be overwhelmed at the prospect of assessing a new home

11. In selecting this site the owners chose a northern exposure for the front facing the street, so that their living area would get a maximum amount of sun from the south. The cluster of dogwood trees by the street was retained when the excavation was done to give depth and interest to the lawn. The site was well graded for good drainage and easy care.

site. An inexpensive pocket compass will help with the directions. Sites can often be visited in different seasons and under different conditions. The dreariest season is late winter when frost is coming out of the ground and mud and running water abound. A site that has possibilities then will seem wonderful in May. In some areas soil conservation agencies and water-shed organizations may be of help. A local naturalist or Audubon member can assess a woodland site by "reading" its plant cover. In many places land use standards are appearing and more should be encouraged.

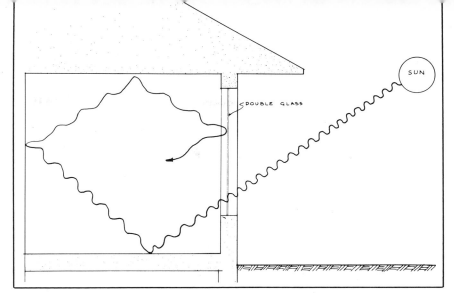

12 (opposite). *Evaluating the inherent qualities of this property early in the planning stage, this home was placed high on a hillside facing south. A natural meadow of clover surrounding it camouflages the vertical rise of the building with the help of a gradually ascending rock garden. The effect is unobtrusive and private. Abundant windows catch the low rays of the winter sun while the trees on the north give protection.*

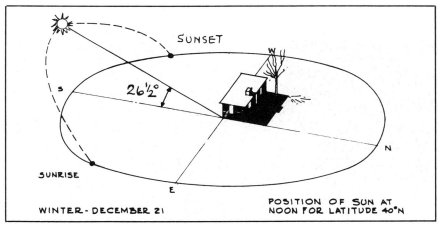

13 (top). *Infra-red rays of the sun entering the room on a short wavelength; inside they are re-radiated on a longer wavelength which cannot escape through the glass.*

14 (center). *The noonday sun of December lies low in the southern sky and casts a deep shadow on the north side of the house.*

15 (bottom). *The noonday sun of June is high in the southern sky and casts a narrow shadow on the north.*

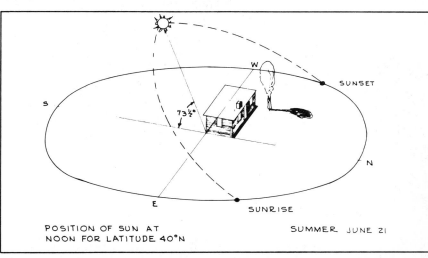

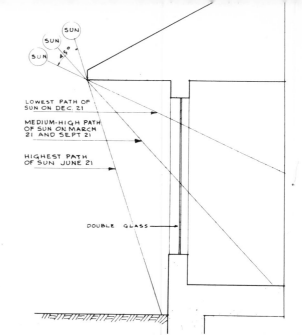

SUN
SUN
SUN 45°

LOWEST PATH OF SUN ON DEC. 21

MEDIUM-HIGH PATH OF SUN ON MARCH 21 AND SEPT 21

HIGHEST PATH OF SUN JUNE 21

DOUBLE GLASS

16. *The low vertical angle of the December sun penetrates deeply into the room with a south window. As the drawing shows, broad overhanging eaves shut out the less-desirable high-angled summer sun.*

17. *Cooling summer breezes sweep up this open southerly slope. A study of air circulation shows that much can be done to relieve stifling summer heat.*

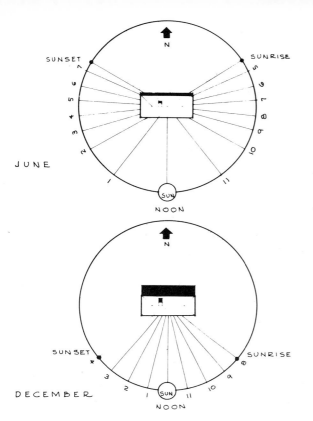

JUNE

SUNSET
7
6
5
4
3
2
1
NOON

N

SUNRISE
5
6
7
8
9
10
11
SUN

DECEMBER

SUNSET
3
2
1
NOON

N

SUNRISE
8
9
10
11
SUN

18. *There is a difference of nearly 60 degrees between the angles of the rising and setting sun of winter and summer.*

19. *Here the house and contour of the land complement each other. Located on a southern slope, the front living area enjoys the most sun, and the rear of the house gets good protection from winter winds.*

II
LAYOUT OF OUTDOOR SPACE

4

PUBLIC SPACE
AND THE ENTRANCE

Most residential properties, from the quarter-acre city or suburban lot to the 25-acre country place, have at least three kinds of outdoor space which can be called public space, service space and outdoor living space. Each of these is usually designated as an area with two dimensions: length and width; but outdoors the sky is the limit and we must become acquainted with a third dimension—height.

THE PUBLIC SPACE

On the small lot, the public space is the portion of the property facing the street. It is bounded by the street, the side property lines and the street facade of the house. (Often the size of this space is prescribed by zoning regulations.) The public space should be a pleasing amalgam of architecture and planting in keeping with the general character of the neighborhood. A neatly shaped foreground of lawn provides the best setting for most residences. If good street trees already exist there may be no need to add more, though a large front lawn may require one or more trees to cast shade as required, to provide shadow patterns on the grass or to balance the architectural mass of the house itself.

While specific planting is not within the scope of this book, a few general suggestions on planting may be useful here. Plants have always been a part of the home scene, and styles have run the gamut from simple colonial to the "foundation jungle." Plants should be used only when they fulfill a need or enhance a structure. Good architecture requires only a few plants of proper form, color and texture, arranged to create a balanced picture of house and landscape, with the entrance the center of interest. Plants may complement good architecture by repeating its lines and masses in different rhythms; they may also be used to correct architectural faults. Tall houses are improved by tall trees about them, or by tall sizeable plants placed outside the corners to broaden the base, and rounded plant forms within the facade. Houses that are long and low are improved by sizeable vertical plants which break up the horizontal lines, by corner planting, and rounded trees about them to soften the lines.

55

Many places are overplanted because people do not realize the ultimate size of the trees and plants nor how fast they grow, eventually shutting out sun and sky. Most modern houses have no visible foundation and hence should not be swathed in plants. The base of a tall house may be widened by side property-line plantings, with a suggestion of planting on the street side to give form to the front lawn. Occasionally, for screen or privacy, the side property lines are solidly planted; in other situations they are less dense to keep front lawns open and shared visually with neighbors. If the most desirable spot for outdoor living is the front yard, it should be screened from the street and developed into private outdoor living space. (See Chapters 9 and 10.)

On old places one may still find an occasional garage located in the backyard. This means one of two things: either the car must be backed down a long side property-line drive to reach the street, or a large amount of space must be given over to a turning area, which hopefully can be screened from the outdoor living area.

Many modern houses have attached garages with driveways coming in directly off the street; the most modest one-car garage usually has a gravel drive with a minimum width of 8 or 9 feet. Guests and tradesmen who must park on the street are happy to have a paved walk 4 feet wide along the drive from the street to the front door. This walk supersedes the one that bisected the front lawn in earlier days.

Wherever possible, off-the-street parking should be part of the public space. Furthermore, it should be adequate for backing and turning so that no car need back out onto the street. The auto requires a vast area for parking and turning around. Even though a homeowner may have only small cars, his parking area should be planned with the average car in mind. The required dimensions are available and it makes good sense to follow them carefully, thus avoiding the aggravation of an inadequate auto court.

Short driveways are best if kept straight since curves confuse the backing process. With more space available the entrance drive can become a delightful experience of subtle curves and neat flowing lines. (Refer to Chapter 12 for help in designing beautiful lines and curves.)

For turning off the street and into the driveway, a minimum radius of 15 feet should be used; if possible make it 20 feet for increased safety. The drive should join the public road at a right angle to provide the best possible visibility in each direction. A single-lane drive should be at least 9 feet wide with an 18-foot minimum for a two-lane drive. When backing out of the garage the front wheels of the car must clear door jambs before the turn can begin. This distance is equal to the wheel base of the car—an average of 10 or 11 feet; the minimum turning radius for the average car is about 18 feet, though 20 feet should be used if possible. For head-in parking a car needs space 9 or10 feet wide and 18 to 20 feet long. An additional clear space of 25 feet should be provided behind a parked car for backing out and turning around.

In our multi-car era a large portion of the public space must often be used for parking. One, two, three and sometimes four family cars must come and go easily and safely, but this does not mean a public space of solid concrete. Useful and attractive space can be designed to accept the auto in a setting of shade trees, evergreens, grass or ground cover. Furthermore, the trip from the parking area to the front entrance may lead through a charming entrance garden.

THE ENTRANCE

An easy and attractive access to the front entrance is just as important as a safe and efficient driveway. The walk to the front entrance should be effortless, but often it is a mystery to be solved (where *is* the front door?), an endurance test, or an obstacle course. There should be no question in a stranger's mind as to the *direction* of the front entrance, even though the door itself may be hidden from sight. If more than one door is visible from the parking area, indicate the front entrance by size, architectural design, or color.

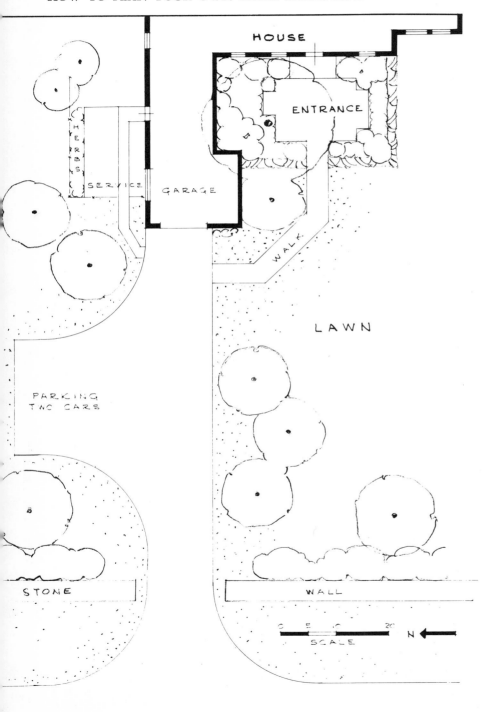

HOUSE

ENTRANCE

H
E
R
B
S

SERVICE   GARAGE

WALK

LAWN

PARKING
TWO CARS

STONE

WALL

SCALE   N

20. *A small house with a one-car garage. The backing and turning slot doubles as a parking space for two guest cars. The walk to the front door is easily distinguished from the service entrance and it leads through a small but attractive entrance garden.*

21. *The front façade is the part of our house that greets the outside world. We like it to be as attractive as possible, with the planting complementing the architecture, giving a feeling of harmony and unity. A foreground of lawn along the street still provides the best setting most of the time.*

The size of the entrance walk and the landing at the front door should be in scale with the house itself. Large houses need generous entrance features which might overwhelm a small house. However, walks, steps and landings are provided to serve people; they should be safe, comfortable, attractive and in scale with human beings. The entrance walk for the smallest of houses should be no less than 4 feet wide; 4½ feet is more comfortable for two persons walking abreast. Larger places may have walks 5 or 6 feet wide. An 8-foot walk will afford space for four people abreast, and is the maximum for large walks. The front entrance walk is no place for stepping stones, no

22. *Most people overplant with the result that their homes are soon lost in horticultural clutter and jungle. Note the clean lines shown here.*

23. *Plants can be used in many ways to complement the architecture. It's always a good rule to keep things simple.*

matter how quaint the architecture; use an all-weather surface without large joints, pitched to drain quickly.

The front entrance landing should be ample enough to accommodate a small group waiting for the bell to be answered or exchanging goodbyes. One would not wish a departing guest to be swept off it by a swinging screen door. The exact size will depend upon the scale of the house; in many cases landings are not adequate in size.

If steps are required between parking area and front entrance, they should be carefully located where people will expect them. Logical spots for steps are at the house landing and at the auto court. These steps should be lighted on the same circuit as the front entrance light. Steps required at other locations should be easily recognized by visitors. Planting, a guide rail, a change of directions or some other device all call attention to unexpected steps. *Never* introduce single steps at odd intervals.

Assuming that steps are properly constructed, their comfort and safety will depend upon the relationship of tread and riser. The *tread* is the flat surface one steps on; the *riser* is the vertical space between treads. Indoors, where space is limited, steps are compact; a 7-inch riser is generally used with a 10½-inch tread. Outdoors, where space is less restricted, a generous 6-inch riser and 12-inch tread are more comfortable and attractive. An even more pleasant effect on a short flight is achieved with 5-inch risers and 13-inch treads. A flight of outdoor steps should be 5 feet wide for the maximum comfort of two persons abreast, though flights 4 feet wide may be used with 4-foot walks. (Consult Chapters 13 and 14 for more information on walks and steps.)

The problems of maintenance deserve consideration. Neat edges make for attractive drives, and if grass and paving are kept at the same elevation the mower can overlap the drive and thus eliminate a separate edging job. (See also Chapter 18.) If a curb *is* used, the top of the curb and the grass should be flush for the same reason. However, northern homeowners need to bear in mind the problem of snow removal. A

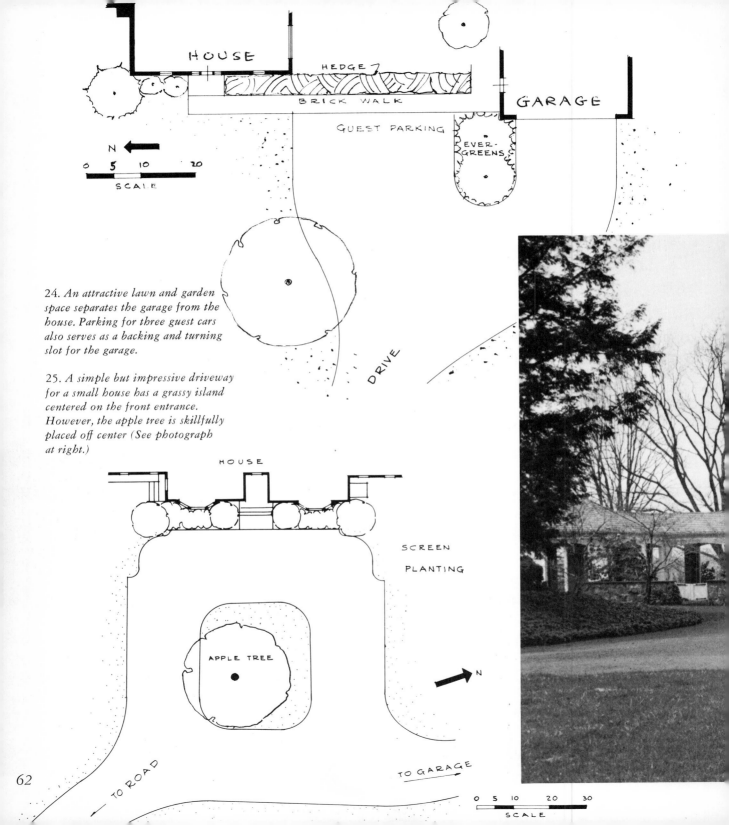

HOUSE

HEDGE

BRICK WALK

GARAGE

GUEST PARKING

EVER-
GREENS

N

0   5   10   20
SCALE

DRIVE

24. *An attractive lawn and garden space separates the garage from the house. Parking for three guest cars also serves as a backing and turning slot for the garage.*

25. *A simple but impressive driveway for a small house has a grassy island centered on the front entrance. However, the apple tree is skillfully placed off center (See photograph at right.)*

HOUSE

SCREEN

PLANTING

APPLE TREE

N

TO ROAD

TO GARAGE

0   5   10   20   30
SCALE

steel or granite block curb can define the driveway and reduce snow-plow damage to the adjoining lawn. Leave a logical snow storage area in grass only and avoid lining the entire drive and parking area with shrubs that would be damaged by snow piled on them. Avoid all planting which could interfere with vision. Good ground cover is safest; it does not need pruning.

26. Wings of the house on both sides are almost like open arms—a warm welcome indeed.

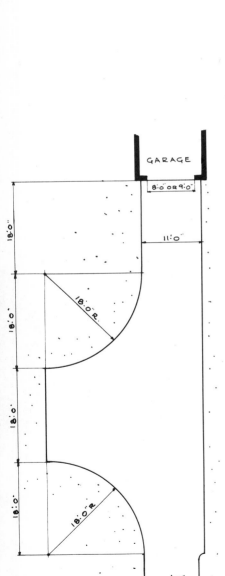

GARAGE

8'·0 OR 9'·0

11'·0

18'·0"

16'·0"

18'·0 R

18'·0'

18'·0'

18'·0 R

10'·0"

27 (left). *Space requirements for backing and turning the average car.*

28 (above). *This illustrates the simple, practical mathematics of driveway space needed to back and turn easily. Other plans may be more elaborate but follow the same basic rules.*

29. *A small house with entrances to the residence and a professional office has a neat parking area developed around an island 24 feet square with curved truncated corners. A handsome dogwood underplanted with myrtle decorates the island and guest cars are parked along the sides.*

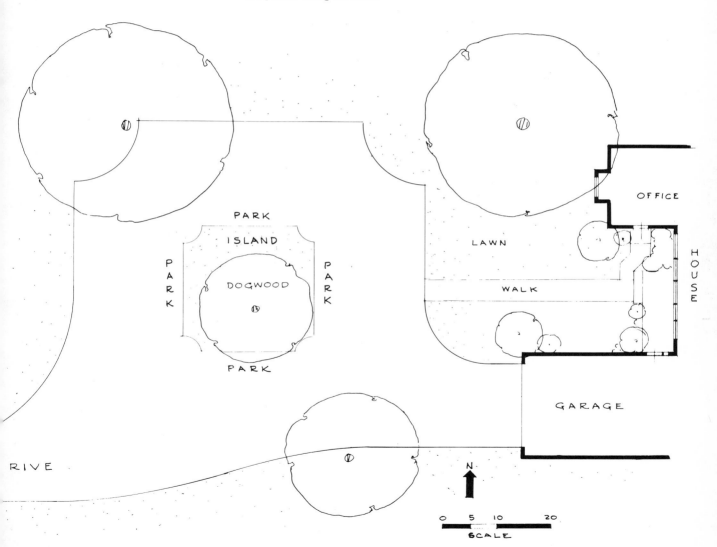

PARK

ISLAND

PARK
PARK

DOGWOOD

PARK

LAWN

WALK

OFFICE

HOUSE

GARAGE

RIVE

N

0   5   10   20
SCALE

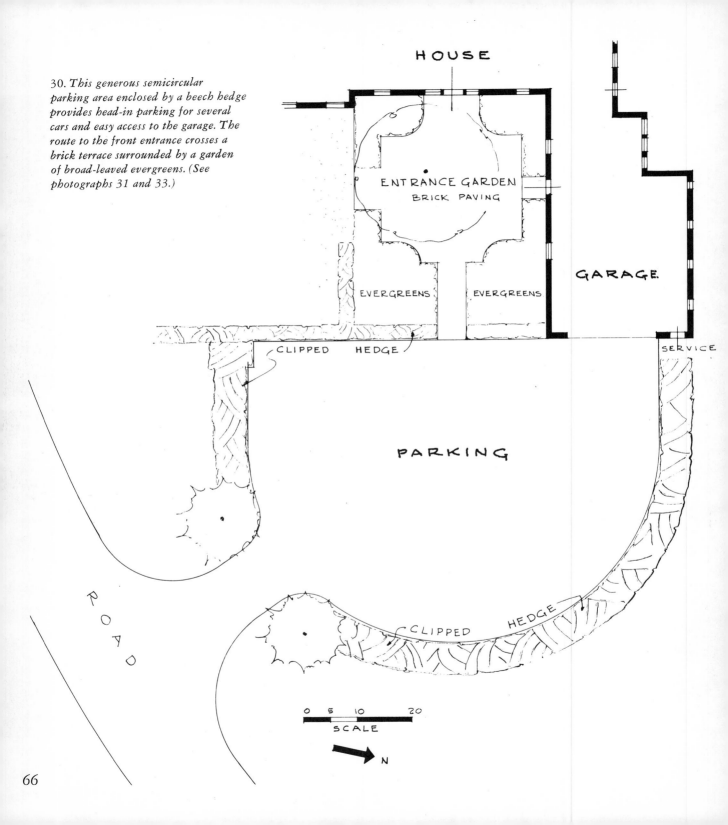

HOUSE

30. *This generous semicircular parking area enclosed by a beech hedge provides head-in parking for several cars and easy access to the garage. The route to the front entrance crosses a brick terrace surrounded by a garden of broad-leaved evergreens. (See photographs 31 and 33.)*

ENTRANCE GARDEN
BRICK PAVING

GARAGE.

EVERGREENS

EVERGREENS

SERVICE

CLIPPED HEDGE

PARKING

CLIPPED HEDGE

ROAD

0 5 10 20
SCALE

N

31. *For a sociable family with entertaining in mind, this parking area can comfortably accommodate a number of cars, all able to back and turn according to the dimension formula given above.*

67

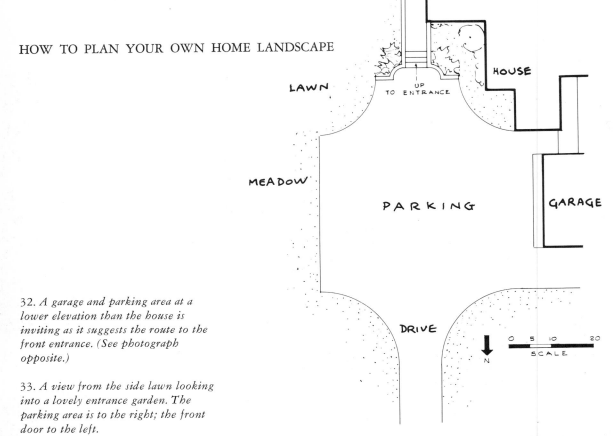

LAWN

HOUSE

UP
TO ENTRANCE

MEADOW

PARKING

GARAGE

DRIVE

0   5   10   20
SCALE

N

32. *A garage and parking area at a lower elevation than the house is inviting as it suggests the route to the front entrance. (See photograph opposite.)*

33. *A view from the side lawn looking into a lovely entrance garden. The parking area is to the right; the front door to the left.*

34. *In this attractive approach, the garage is hidden by the trees on the right.*

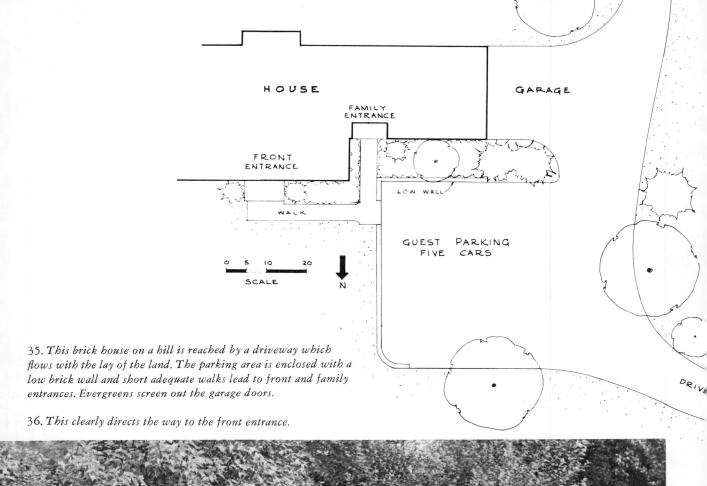

HOUSE

GARAGE

FAMILY
ENTRANCE

FRONT
ENTRANCE

LOW WALL

WALK

GUEST   PARKING
FIVE   CARS

0   5   10   20

SCALE

N

DRIVE

35. *This brick house on a hill is reached by a driveway which flows with the lay of the land. The parking area is enclosed with a low brick wall and short adequate walks lead to front and family entrances. Evergreens screen out the garage doors.*

36. *This clearly directs the way to the front entrance.*

37. *An entrance to a front door should be effortless—no cumbersome steps to climb, no wet grass to walk through. A considerate front entrance is like a warm welcome.*

38. *A front landing should be in scale with the dimensions of the house and large enough for several people. If shelter from rain and snow is possible, it will be greatly appreciated.*

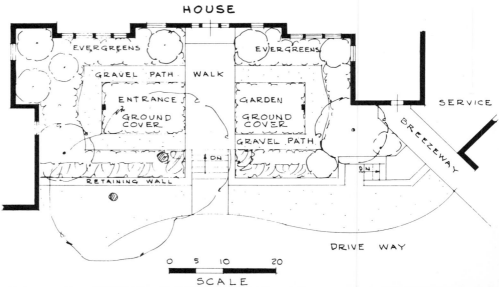

HOUSE

EVERGREENS   EVERGREENS

GRAVEL PATH   WALK

ENTRANCE   GARDEN

GROUND COVER   GROUND COVER

GRAVEL PATH

SERVICE

BREEZEWAY

DN   DN

RETAINING WALL

DRIVE WAY

0   5   10   20

SCALE

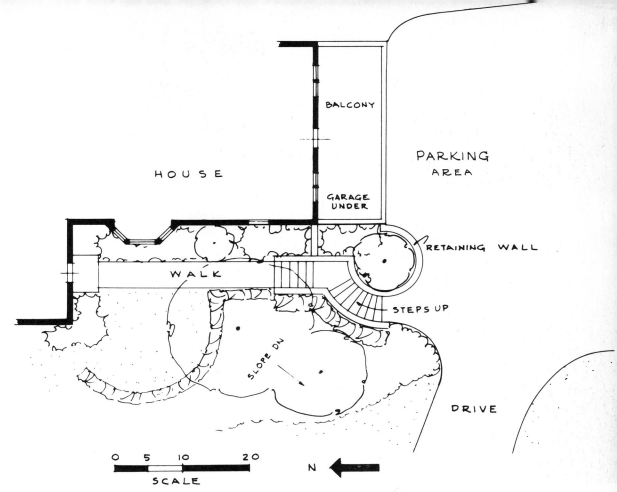

BALCONY

PARKING AREA

HOUSE

GARAGE UNDER

RETAINING WALL

WALK

STEPS UP

SLOPE DN

DRIVE

0   5   10   20
SCALE

N

40. *On sites with considerable change of grade the garage and parking area may be at a lower level than the house. This may present problems of access to the front entrance (all too often solved by a narrow flight of steep concrete steps). Here the steps are a part of the entrance garden: easy steps with adequate handrails follow the circular fieldstone wall supporting a small flowering tree, evergreens and ground cover. This takes the visitor to a landing, followed by a second short easy flight. The circular theme is repeated in a grass panel formed with low evergreens separating the lawn from the steep planted slope.*

39 (opposite). *This house, on a sloping site, has the main entrance at a lower level than the drive. An easy flight of steps and a broad entrance walk lead to the front door. Since grass would be difficult to maintain, the planting consists of evergreen ground cover beds surrounded by broad-leaved evergreens and two small flowering trees, all adding up to an enticing entrance garden.*

41. *An entrance drive can become a delightful experience with subtle curves and neat flowing lines. Curbed edges make maintenance easier and also accentuate the curve line.*

42. *On a steep slope the logical parking area is at the side of the house, convenient to the front entrance for guests and to the kitchen entrance for the family.*

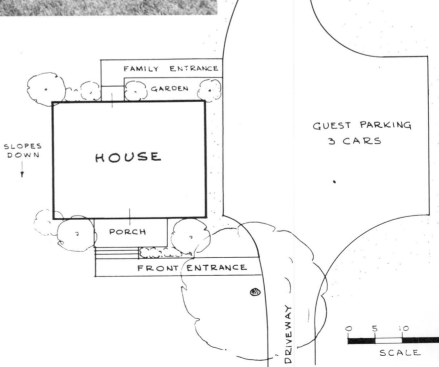

TO GARAGE

FAMILY ENTRANCE

GARDEN

GUEST PARKING
3 CARS

SLOPES
DOWN

HOUSE

PORCH

FRONT ENTRANCE

DRIVEWAY

0 5 10

SCALE

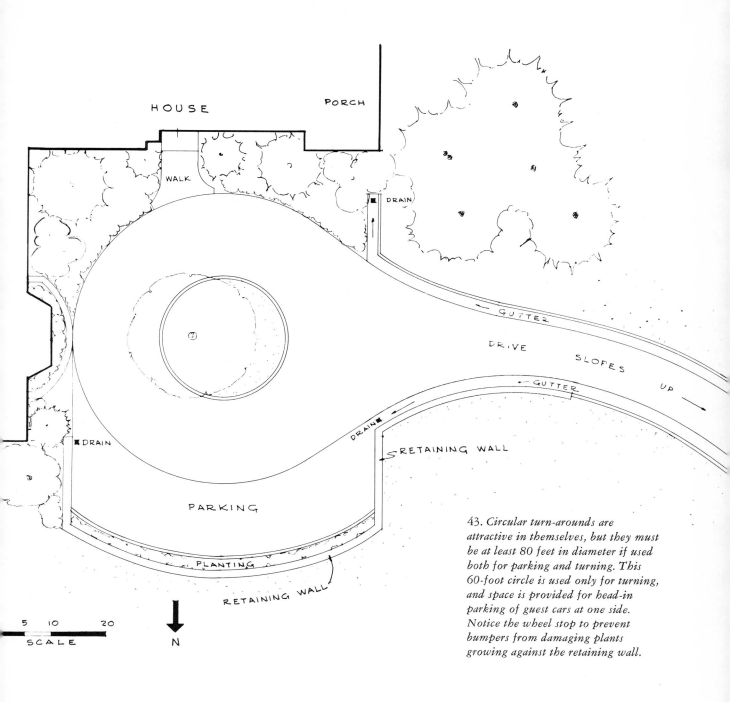

HOUSE

PORCH

WALK

DRAIN

GUTTER

DRIVE SLOPES UP

GUTTER

DRAIN

RETAINING WALL

DRAIN

PARKING

PLANTING

RETAINING WALL

5 10 20

SCALE

N

43. Circular turn-arounds are
attractive in themselves, but they must
be at least 80 feet in diameter if used
both for parking and turning. This
60-foot circle is used only for turning,
and space is provided for head-in
parking of guest cars at one side.
Notice the wheel stop to prevent
bumpers from damaging plants
growing against the retaining wall.

75

5

SERVICE
AND STORAGE SPACE

The well-planned landscape should provide adequate service space which need not be large if it's well planned and properly located. An already overloaded garage is not the proper place to store broken bicycles, pots of faded Easter lilies and bags of Bovung.

A conveniently located screened-off service yard will accommodate garbage and trash—universal problems even with disposal and compacting equipment. More and more of our waste must be recycled to reduce the glut as well as to conserve dwindling resources. Lightweight plastic containers, one for each type (glass, paper, aluminum, etc.), may be stored in a utility bin with a labelled lift-up cover over each container and a door on the front of the bin for easy removal. These are best on a base of concrete or asphalt, and the entire unit should be served by an all-weather walk from the kitchen door.

Though indoor dryers are nearly universal, a permanent or a pullout clothes-line for sunning and airing woolens and for occasional drying should be included in the service yard.

Storage for outdoor equipment, tools and supplies—firewood, bicycles, outdoor furniture, wheeled toys, mowing and leaf-gathering equipment, fertilizing and spraying materials, garden tools, hose and watering devices—requires an alarming amount of space, which can be provided in several ways. A lean-to extension of the garage can include a workbench and provide organized storage. A separate tool shed/ storage building may double as a feature in the landscape. In other situations storage units or prefabricated storage walls can be built or installed against an existing house or garage wall, under a roof over-hang or as free-standing units. In fact, the service yard itself can be formed of storage units with the solid back walls of each unit serving as a section of the enclosing fence, with all doors opening into the service yard. Specific space is provided for each piece of equipment or item to be stored. Tools can have their outlines painted on the wall behind them.

If there is a gardener in the family, the service yard should contain 77 bins for topsoil, sand, peat moss, fertilizer, flower pots, a waist-high potting bench, and a hose bibb; even a cold frame can be included. The service yard fence may be designed with slatted shelves and an overhead lath sun-screen to provide summer quarters for house plants. Furthermore, there may be room for raised garden beds, enclosed by railroad ties or 2-by-12 boards on edge, where herbs, salad greens, tomatoes, or something of special interest can be grown. If no other spot is available, the compost bin can be added here.

The service yard is most useful with a smooth all-weather surface of concrete or asphalt, though a wellmade gravel surface is acceptable. Paved service yards can double as play areas for wheeled toys, hopscotch courts and even basketball practice.

Since many garden materials arrive by truck or family station wagon, the service space should be accessible from the driveway. A double-leaf gate with a minimum width of 8 feet is worth considering. A single gate should be 4 feet wide to permit passage of a wheelbarrow without scraping the gardener's knuckles.

Consider how this area will look from the entrance drive. The usual laundry fence quickly identifies a service yard. If the public side is converted into a clematis arbor or used as a background for espaliered fruits it becomes a feature in itself. A clipped evergreen hedge may screen out the service yard. If it adjoins the garage, a fence or wall of the same material and color as the garage can also act as camouflage.

An enthusiastic gardener needs more growing space than raised beds in a service yard. The paved enclosed yard should be reserved for general service use and the gardener given his due. This can be a sunny space with good soil, accessible from the service yard, perhaps even an extension of it, which may be developed into a working garden. It can be small and compact if well designed, with neat beds separated by walks of gravel, brick or pine needles, supported by a wood or metal curb. The feature of interest may be a tool or lath house with a small work terrace, comfortable benches, and a dipping well, shaded by a grape arbor. If space is no problem, there can be an asparagus bed or a berry patch. Most certainly there will be a compost pile. This working garden should be carefully located and sufficiently screened so that it need not be unattractive in winter. Bear in mind that a pleasant pattern of garden beds and walks have enough form to be of some interest, even without plants.

With the high cost of meat, some homeowners are growing their own. A shelter for a few hens or broilers or a hutch for rabbits requires little space, in or near the service yard. A tethered lamb can double as lawn mower during the day, but needs a safe enclosure by night. A pet pig needs a tight fence and no nearby neighbors.

CHILDREN'S PLAY AREAS

Play areas for small children can be provided almost everywhere; they should not be considered permanent, since interests change from year to year. Fences should be easily installed and removed, since a two-year-old will require a different enclosure than a child of four. Small children are happy with a portable sandbox and a plastic wading pool nearby, where they can see parents and be seen by them. A swing can be attached to a nearby tree limb; an apple tree is great for climbing, and it shades the sandbox at the same time.

A single low-branched tree or clump of bushes becomes a lookout, a hideway, a house with rooms and endless furnishings. A big tree with good loose earth beneath it provides endless possibilities for creative manipulation, destruction and construction plus an important sensory experience of modeling earth and mud.

Small children's play areas can be converted into gardens when children no longer need them and when parents have more time for gardening.

Walks, garage courts and service yards are good for use of bikes and a garage court can double as a basketball court; in the meantime it can also serve for hopscotch and roller skating.

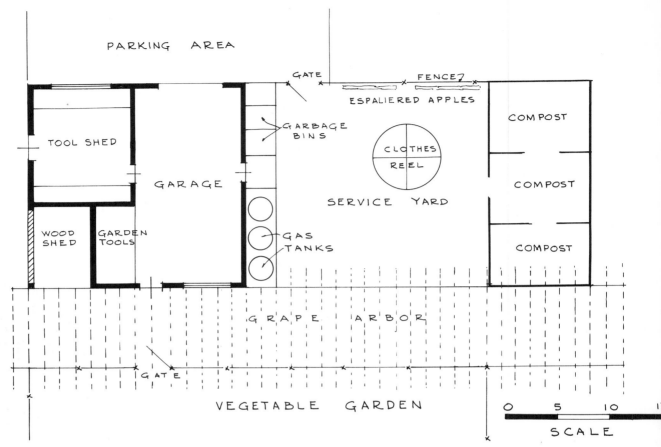

PARKING AREA

TOOL SHED

GARAGE

GATE

FENCE

ESPALIERED APPLES

GARBAGE BINS

COMPOST

CLOTHES REEL

COMPOST

SERVICE YARD

WOOD SHED

GARDEN TOOLS

GAS TANKS

COMPOST

GRAPE ARBOR

GATE

VEGETABLE GARDEN

0   5   10   15

SCALE

44. *A compact service yard beside the garage is also convenient to the garden.*

45. *Off the kitchen door, a vine-covered areaway screens off storage areas for various items (such as tools) not for show.*

46 (left). *A convenient closed-off service yard is very useful. Garbage cans and such things are handily tucked away behind the openwork wall of concrete block. Covered with a clematis vine or otherwise suitably planted, one would never suspect this small yard of its functional purpose.*

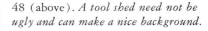

47 (left). *Firewood, cut and stored and protected from the weather, is ready for use on cold wintry nights.*

48 (above). *A tool shed need not be ugly and can make a nice background.*

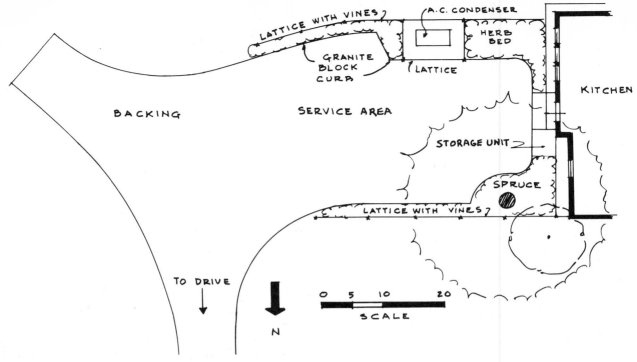

LATTICE WITH VINES

A.C. CONDENSER

HERB
BED

GRANITE
BLOCK
CURB

LATTICE

KITCHEN

BACKING

SERVICE AREA

STORAGE UNIT

SPRUCE

LATTICE WITH VINES

TO DRIVE

0 5 10 20
SCALE

N

49. Service areas may be assets rather than liabilities if carefully planned. This one off the end of the house is completely screened by two lines of latticework fencing in a diamond-shaped pattern planned to support a collection of clematis. The air-conditioner compressor is also enclosed with lattice. There is a small herb garden and one or two cars can be parked while delivery trucks come and go.

50. A separate tool or potting shed is a great help to the serious gardener. Bags of fertilizer, seeds, rakes and hoes are where you want them. The invaluable compost pile should be close by.

51. *A vegetable and herb enthusiast might use the space just outside the back door as a small kitchen garden.*

52. *The chicken run is inconspicuously placed behind the tool shed.*

6

SITTING SPACE

The American house of the past was built with the parlor and sitting room facing the street, and the kitchen, laundry and service porch at the rear. Alas, far too many of today's houses still have the living room with its picture window overlooking the street. A more pleasant relationship is possible if living areas open out on the private part of the property so there can be free movement between indoor living rooms and the outdoors—whether terrace, patio, court, lawn or garden. Thus, outdoor living becomes intimately related to indoor living.

Excellent information is available on how to build a wide variety of outdoor features, but there is very little help for the layman in the way of guidelines for the most important first steps—the analysis and planning that must precede building.

PORCHES AND TERRACES

The most popular outdoor feature is the sitting area. In places where insects are a problem, proper use of yellow lights will discourage them at night, and smoke is an effective repellent, but the only complete control is screening. Porches look best when planned as part of the house rather than just "tacked on"; if they are placed at the end of a wing where breezes blow through, they may be oases of coolness in hot weather. Some porches are designed with interchangeable panels of screening and glass which greatly extend the period of usefulness. A porch should have easy access to the main terrace, providing another point of interchange between covered and uncovered sitting space. If there is no place for a screened porch and if sitting out is sheer misery because of insects, then consider a separate screened structure and treat it as a feature in the garden.

BUILDING A TERRACE

In many homes the terrace is a do-it-yourself project representing a tremendous amount of work and considerable money. If it is to be worth the effort, one should answer the following questions in advance: 85

Where should it be placed? How large should it be? What shape should it have? What kind of surface does it need?

The main terrace, to be used for entertaining as well as other family needs, should be closely related to the living areas of the house; in fact, its usefulness is in direct proportion to its proximity. In less humid climates the main terrace may be of the same paving material and at the same level as the house floor, but in eastern United States, at least one step down is important in keeping out the weather. Steps here must be an easy generous outdoor ratio; for safety and comfort, risers should have a maximum height of 6 inches for treads 12 inches wide. Combinations of 5-inch risers with 13-inch treads or 4-inch risers with 14-inch treads should be considered, if space permits. Steps should be wider than the door itself. In modern houses with several sliding glass doors the outdoor steps may extend across the entire expanse of doors as a transitional feature serving the eye as well as the feet.

It is not always easy to add a workable terrace to older houses with high foundations; sometimes the main floor level is 3 or 4 feet above ground level. The only access to the outside may be the front door and the kitchen door; a trip through the kitchen and laundry and down the back stairs to the outdoor sitting area is not good enough. Perhaps a living room window can be changed into a pair of French doors to provide more direct access; a stretch of wall may be replaced with a plate glass window to improve the visual relationship between indoors and outdoors. However, a steep flight of steps to the terrace below is a deterrent as well as a potential hazard. If high foundations are the problem, one may install a wooden deck at the house floor level or one step below, as an alternative to raising the grade with earth fill and retaining walls to support a terrace. Sometimes the deck may serve as a transitional feature used for seating small groups and as a passageway to a larger terrace below. Houses on very steep terrain may use decks rather than ground level terraces for outdoor sitting. Duckboard is an ideal flooring, for water runs right through it. It is usually constructed of 2-by-4's nailed flat onto floor joists with enough separation to let rain through. An existing tree can be incorporated in the deck itself, providing immediate shade and a feature of unusual interest.

In situations where both the living room and the best exposure for outdoor living face the street, the logical conclusion is to convert all of the front space, except that part actually needed for the entrance, into an outdoor living room, enclosed and screened from the street and driveway. (See Chapter 9.)

Eating and drinking are a part of outdoor living. A separate dining terrace near the source of food or a cook-out spot removed from the house both serve the purpose. In other homes a large living terrace serves a double function: the portion nearest the kitchen or dining room is used for dining, while the larger portion is reserved for lounging. To be used to its maximum the dining area must have easy access to the kitchen; negotiating a number of steps with a heavy tray diminishes one's enthusiasm for eating out. The dining terrace should be large enough to accommodate a weatherproof table, chairs or benches, and still be large enough to allow diners to circulate without stepping off the terrace. A serving table against the house wall with electric outlets for warming equipment is a real help. Breakfast, lunch and afternoon tea are all pleasant outdoors—a sheltered location, comfortable chairs and an agreeable view provide the ideal setting.

Additional outdoor sitting areas should be added as needed. A bedroom may have its own private terrace. A spot near the family entrance becomes a small work terrace for a variety of tasks—arranging flowers, preparing vegetables or doing special cleaning jobs. Other sitting areas may be completely divorced from the house itself: a terrace at the playhouse or pool for teenage parties, or a charming picnic area of flat fieldstones laid level with the grass under an old apple tree. Each family will have its favorites according to season or time of day.

Where shall the terrace be placed? If it is to be used often, it must be convenient to the living portion of the house and must also be comfortable enough for extended outdoor use: cool in summer yet sunny and cozy in chilly weather. How can one location serve all needs?

Depending on local conditions, a terrace on the south or southeast side of the house may be reasonably comfortable in hot and in cool weather *if* shade from deciduous trees or overhead vines is added to control the sunlight. (See Chapter 16.) An eastern terrace can be very useful; it is warm and sunny in the early morning and shaded by the house during the hottest part of the afternoon. A bit of planting can divert summer breezes across the terrace; a part of the house or garage can screen the north winds in spring and fall. A terrace with southwest exposure will have air circulation but needs careful shading in the afternoon during hot weather. Western terraces are often too hot to be useful in late afternoon when they are most needed, yet they may have high priority because of a view or the enjoyment that comes with watching a sunset. Well-placed planting can reduce the heat problem, though not always solve it completely. Though a terrace which faces north is least desirable for year-round use, it can have certain advantages. It is very pleasant to sit on a north terrace and look into a landscape and garden flooded with sunlight—since flowers turn their faces to the sun they will also be turning their faces to the observer. In addition, a north view is restful because there is less glare.

A sun trap for winter use can often be arranged. Sun traps, out of the wind, where the sun's radiant heat can be concentrated, absorbed and reflected are wonderful outdoor sitting areas. In a south-facing angle of the house the midday temperature can register 70 degrees even though the lawn a few feet away is covered with snow. Dark flagstone paving which absorbs heat, and white house walls which concentrate and reflect it, make this June-in-January spot a very workable idea.

Where then should the terrace be placed? A good answer would be to have several outdoor sitting areas for different moods and temperatures. If only one is possible, let it be south, southeast, or east of the house, and "manage" the sunlight as required for comfort.

What size should the terrace be? One landscape architect suggests that it be "large enough so that guests won't back into the flower beds but small enough so it doesn't resemble a parking lot." One must consider its relationship both to the house and to the total outdoor living space. This is a matter of scale and the same yardstick does not work indoors and out—features designed for indoor use look too small outdoors. It is important that the main terrace used for entertaining be larger than the living room, because it is used in a larger, freer, more energetic way than similar space indoors. A small house may be considerably improved by the addition of a well-designed, well-placed terrace which extends and enlarges the house, both from within and without. Definite rules are not always wise, but for practical reasons a terrace should be at least 16 feet wide if at all possible; since most terraces are used for traffic as well as for sitting, part will be used as a walkway from the door to other parts of the property. Recognize this traffic pattern and keep it open. In any event, the terrace should accommodate the number of people who regularly use it. A paved terrace seating a dozen people comfortably can be used for a larger number if it is open to the lawn at the same level on the front or sides, enabling guests to move off the paving and onto the surrounding grass.

What form or shape shall the terrace have? Since many terraces are of masonry and represent a considerable investment, they must be not only practical but aesthetically pleasing as well.

Most houses are made up of straight lines, distinct angles and geometric curves. Any feature closely related to architecture should similarly have form as opposed to being formless. This does not imply that it be stiff or formal; form is the quality that pleases the eye and eases the soul, and therefore it plays an important role in even the most casual space division.

The main terrace adjacent or closely related to the house needs a clean, strong, satisfying form of good proportions in scale with the house and nearby outdoor space. No one form is right for all terraces, for form should evolve from the available space; it may repeat an architectural detail or echo the contour of a nearby land form. A terrace may be rectangular, square, circular, octagonal, spiral, elliptical or free-form.

Our civilized life has a background of rectangularity, or straight lines and right angles in streets, houses, rooms, furniture, books and hundreds of everyday things. Thus it is easy to see why the majority of terraces in close proximity to houses are also rectangular. However, rectangles vary greatly; some are long and narrow, others short and wide. Some have pleasant proportions, others not. How can one be sure of a well-proportioned rectangle?

In design there is a ratio, borrowed from nature, known as the "golden mean." Simply stated, it is the relationship of 1 to 1.618. If 1 represents the width of a rectangle and 1.618 the length, the result is a golden mean rectangle. (For the non-mathematical this ratio can be simplified as 10 feet of width to 16 feet of length). Unlike the ancients who had to construct this rectangle on the ground, we can solve it by simple arithmetic. Suppose we consider a terrace with a width of 16 feet. How long should this terrace be? Using the golden mean ratio its length should be 25½ feet. Now suppose we have a length of 20 feet in which to build a terrace. How wide should it be? Again using the golden mean ratio, we arrive at 12½ feet, the ideal width for a terrace 20 feet long.

Although there are many occasions when length or width needs adjustment, most ungainly rectangular forms will be avoided by working somewhere within this framework. While a nicely proportioned rectangular terrace is a joy to behold, something less conventional may be more interesting and just as appropriate. Terraces of special interest result from simple variations on the rectangular theme. Sometimes one corner may be replaced by a generous curve, emphasizing a view, or suggesting the direction for a pleasant stroll in the garden.

A square is more static and less interesting than a rectangle, yet square areas are often logical spots for terraces. The area may be surrounded on three sides by the house with strong emphasis in one direction. Or a square terrace may be located in the angle of a house, giving it two lines of sight. A third situation is a square terrace in the angle of a house with a strong diagonal sight line which suggests rounding off the outside corner so that the eye may slip beyond it easily. Like the rectangle, the square form can be modified by special corner treatment and by surface patterns in the paving.

Circles and portions of circles are free, easy, relaxed outdoor forms used abundantly in nature. A circular terrace relieves the hard straight lines of the house yet has a strong simple form in its own right. A

53. The favorite outdoor feature today is the terrace—where your hospitality moves outdoors or where you just relax and let the world roll by. Good terraces should not be placed at random: considerations of sun, prevailing winds and privacy are paramount. (See drawing 8.)

circle tucked into a corner gives a feeling of security. A circular terrace overlooking a view encourages the viewer to feast his eyes on the complete panorama; the eye is not tripped by the edge, but glides easily over the curving border. Or a circular form may be wrapped around the corner of the house, providing two different exposures for the sitter. Sometimes a large circular or semi-circular terrace is dictated by the form of the land as it falls away from the house.

Another useful form is the octagon—a cross between a square and a circle, more interesting than a square yet less difficult to shape in masonry than a circle.

The free-form or spiral is beautiful when thoughtfully designed. It gives a feeling of informality yet it is alive, dynamic and dramatic, lending itself especially well to modern houses. The larger portion can be an accent or can relate to a view, the important part of the house or a spot of natural shade. The narrower portion—or stem—of this terrace may serve as circulation; the widened portion is the full-blown flower. Careful design must go into this terrace. It should be staked out on the ground before any actual work is begun. Not only is the form important, but the boundary line of the terrace must be beautiful in itself. (Since the flowing curved line appears in many parts of the landscape, its design is discussed in Chapter 12.)

The materials of terrace construction: These vary widely and are partly a matter of preference. Both for minimum maintenance and maximum use, at least one terrace (preferably the main one) should be paved with an all-weather surface. It should be smooth and level with the smallest joints possible so that furniture does not wobble. Nothing is more annoying than having high heels and table legs slip into wide cracks between stones. Sometimes the homeowner uses irregular flagstones with grass joints in hopes that this will help to break up the expanse of paving, but grass joints soon develop into ridges separating the stones. The uneven surface makes it impossible to find a level spot for furniture, and during a shower each stone becomes a small well which collects and holds water. Furthermore, the terrace soon develops into a maintenance problem since the lawn mower shears off the top of the grassy ridges leaving untidy bits to be clipped by hand. Then there are those terraces literally clothed with rock garden plants growing between the stones, so that one must wander through a jungle of sedum and basket of gold searching for an unplanted spot on which to sit or stand.

Good materials for terrace construction vary locally. The commonly available ones include brick and medium-gray flagstone (squares and rectangles of varying sizes) laid with the smallest possible space between stones. Both stone and brick may be laid dry on a drainage base of sand or rock dust or, for more permanence, on a concrete foundation. Concrete (tinted to reduce the glare) is less hot underfoot than flagstone, but is usually considered less interesting than other materials. However, a variety of textured effects and finishes can take away the plain concrete look. In addition, there are endless combinations of brick, stone and concrete so that every homeowner can be his own designer. One should resist the temptation to use wood rounds as surfacing materials, at least for the main terrace, since they present problems with the interstices. By the same token do not use irregular flagstones unless they are laid on concrete, with concrete between the joints. The form of the paving and its surface pattern should make a balanced composition. As a means of space division the paving should add interest and pattern, but with simplicity: if it detracts from the view or the surrounding garden it is overdone.

The hard bare look of paving may be softened in a number of ways. A band of planting between the house and the terrace is usually a pleasant feature and a bed here helps reduce glare and heat which could be reflected into the house. It may contain low evergreens to give form and color in winter with space to tuck in spring-flowering bulbs and a few sturdy summer annuals, later replaced by chrysanthemums for autumn. With a masonry house, it is pleasant to have this bed raised above the terrace level; if it is enclosed by a wall 15 inches high with a generous coping, it becomes a pleasant spot for sitting. Planting between paving stones should be limited to a narrow ribbon of moss on shady terraces or, for sunny spots a bit of prostrate thyme which tolerate trampling. Avoid succulent plants such as sedum which are slippery underfoot. For terrace decoration, much can be said for plotted plants in attractive containers. If desired, built-in planting beds or boxes can be a part of the terrace design. For an intimately related combination of garden and terrace refer to Chapter 9.

There is a great deal to be said for grass terraces, especially those located outside large glass surfaces that face south. Grass reflects less heat and glare into the house and is cooler than any paving. On the debit side, it cannot be used when the surface is wet or the ground soft; the maintenance is also higher because of wear. Grass is less satisfactory for the intensive use of terrace furniture. A good compromise is a paved sitting area with lawn beyond it at the same level. The paving serves for intensive all-weather use and the adjoining grass is really an overflow terrace. This also gives a feeling of openness and extension— good impressions to cultivate on a small place.

Sometimes a dramatic effect is produced by keeping the terrace higher than the surrounding land. If the paving is one easy riser above the lawn and if the outer edge of the terrace is a gentle curve, it is an invitation to look and walk out into the lawn and garden. A terrace more than 8 inches above the lawn must have steps for safe descent. A slight change of grade can be a delight and the necessary steps a bit of garden sculpture, guiding the eye as well as the feet in continuing the line of sight from the door or main window. Make such steps broad and generous, with easy risers and wide treads. In places where steps detract from the desired restful character they may be placed to one side or in a corner.

Terraces raised above the surrounding grade need some kind of enclosure to prevent accidents. This can create a feeling of restriction and should be kept as low as possible. A wall 15 inches above terrace level is pleasant and may double as a sitting wall if there is a wide coping. A pierced wall of brick or 4-inch wide concrete block gives some feeling of openness. Sometimes a band of low planting along the outer edge of the terrace will suffice, or a hedge can be planted on the lower level and clipped to form a green parapet. Any planting or construction on the outer edge of the terrace visually cuts off a portion of the land directly in front and hence makes the remaining space seem smaller than it actually is.

A paved terrace also represents masonry that reflects glare and heat when the sun shines on it. The darker the paving material, the more heat it absorbs on a summer day. Not only is the paving hot underfoot, it heats the surrounding air and indirectly the house and the terrace user as well. Light-colored paving materials reflect sunlight and heat and so are less hot in themselves. However, this reflected sunlight is very glaring. It is best to choose medium-colored paving materials and to intercept the sunlight that falls on it during the hottest season.

Shading the terrace: There are many ways of providing intermittent shade at certain hours of the day; most of these are based on the varying angles at which the sun rises and sets and the height of the sun above the horizon at noon. Narrow adjustable louvres can control sun and shade at will, while an overheated structure of wide-fixed louvres lets sun through when it is high in the sky and restricts it at other hours.

Even better devices for producing shade are those that use plants. The bare trellis, exposed to the fierce summer sun, may reach temperatures well over 100 degrees, but if it is covered with a green vine which reflects much of the sun's heat and gives off an unbelievable quantity of moisture, the leafy bower will be only a few degrees hotter than the air temperature. The space below the arbor is not only shaded but actually cooler than it would be without a vine. What happier arrangement than to use a deciduous vine that drops its leaves in autumn, so that the winter sun comes through unobstructed.

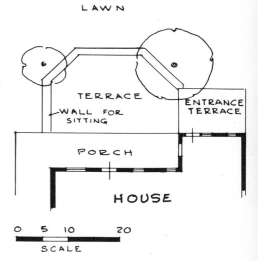

54. *The narrow screened porch on a small cottage was supplemented by a terrace, made possible by a stone retaining wall since the land slopes away from the house. The top of the wall, 15 inches above the paving, serves as additional sitting space. The small entrance terrace handles the traffic to and from the house. Two trees provide shade.*

95

55. Just three short steps from the living room, this terrace charmingly accommodates additional guests at large parties, and is a lovely setting for a few friends at tea time when good weather beckons. Cool in the summer with a central shade tree, it's sunny and warm in the spring and fall.

Undoubtedly the most valuable shading device for a terrace is one or more well-placed deciduous trees. Not only do they shade the terrace during the hottest hours of the day, they also shade the house walls and part of the roof. Their enormous areas of leaf surface provide radiant air cooling as they evaporate gallons of water through the process of transpiration. This cooled air moves downward, refreshing those sitting underneath the trees. (This is discussed in more detail in Chapter 16.)

Trees help to solve the problem of glare, too. Second only to the sun itself, the whitish summer sky is a fierce glare-producer. By using trees as a green overhead canopy to shut out some of the sky, the glare is greatly reduced. Underneath this canopy one sees the lawn and view

which reflect a gentle, less glaring, indirect light. A modern house with a great expanse of glass may use a green canopy of clipped tree foliage to reduce the glare.

Do not hesitate to use trees in the paved terrace itself. With adequate soil preparations and wise choice of varieties they will grow almost as well as trees in the lawn. Choose those with straight clean trunks and place them so that you do not look directly into a trunk from a window or door. Keep the lower limbs pruned to allow for walking underneath. Adequate openings surrounding the trunk may have ground cover plants. Paved terraces built around existing trees will need special attention in order to preserve the tree.

56. Deck terraces are a good solution to grading problems. A step down onto the terrace is important to keep the weather out of the house, and a flooring of duckboard lets water run through. An existing tree makes an interesting feature here and, of course, keeps the terrace cool in summer.

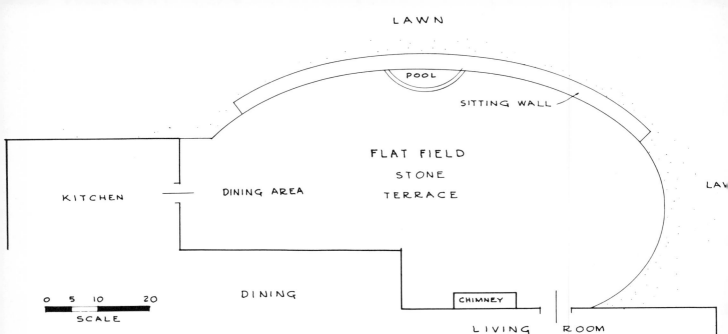

LAWN

POOL

SITTING WALL

FLAT FIELD
STONE
TERRACE

KITCHEN

DINING AREA

LAW

DINING

CHIMNEY

LIVING   ROOM

0 5 10   20
SCALE

57. *A sizeable terrace beside an old farm house is bordered on one side by a low fieldstone wall which supports the existing lawn at a higher elevation; it is also the right height for a sitting wall. The portion near the kitchen is convenient for dining out.*

58. *This brick dining terrace is fan-shaped to accentuate the expanding view. (See drawing 60.)*

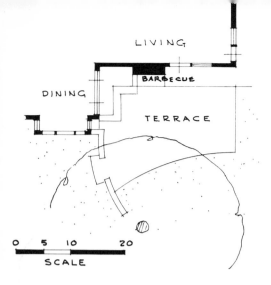

LIVING

BARBECUE

DINING

TERRACE

0 5 10 20
SCALE

59. *An existing barbecue area was improved by an adequate paved terrace and a low sitting wall of brick. A huge oak provides shade.*

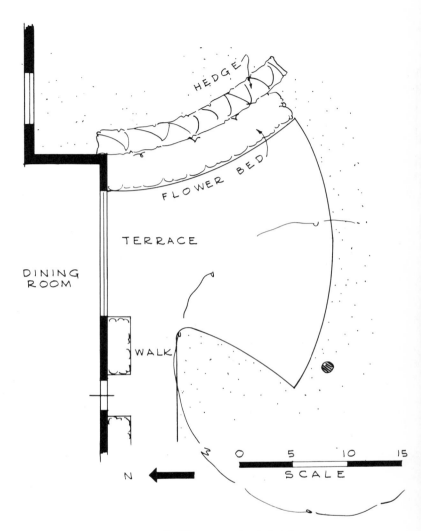

HEDGE

FLOWER BED

DINING ROOM

TERRACE

WALK

N

0 5 10 15
SCALE

60. *The terrace is shaded by a sugar maple and bordered by a tiny garden of tulips, annuals and chrysanthemums, with a holly hedge for background.*

99

61. *A terrace built among existing trees is usable over a long season because of its orientation. The portion close to the house, protected from the northwest wind and open to the sun, is comfortable in fall and spring and even on a warm winter day. This protected portion sweeps out into a broad circular summer terrace, open to the summer breeze and a view of the pond.*

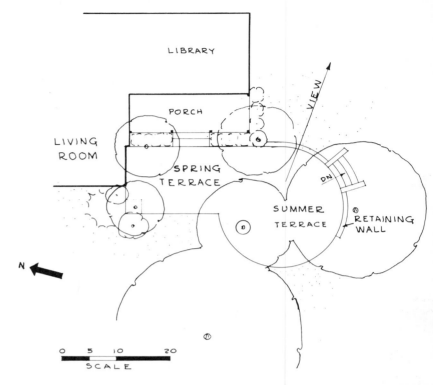

LIBRARY

PORCH

LIVING ROOM

SPRING TERRACE

VIEW

DN

SUMMER TERRACE

RETAINING WALL

N

0   5   10   20
SCALE

62 (below). *This is a cool spot—an open room in which shade-loving plants and people can escape the blistering hot sun.*

63 and 64 (above and right). *This
free-form terrace provides access from
both living room and library and is a
pleasant unifying shape for an angular
situation. It will accommodate a large
group because paving and lawn are
at the same level.*

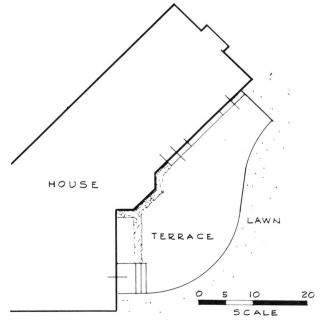

HOUSE

TERRACE

LAWN

0   5   10   20
SCALE

GOLDEN MEAN RECTANGLE

W = 1.0
(10)

L =   1.618 (16)

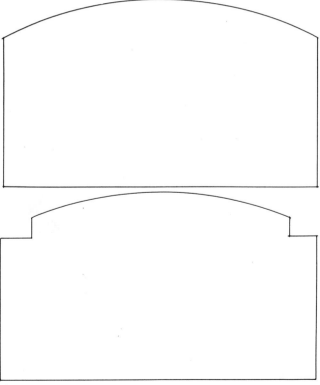

65. *The golden mean rectangle has a width of 1.0 and a length of 1.618. For easy arithmetic this ratio can be expressed as 10:16. (See page 90.)*

66. *For variety a golden mean rectangle can be bowed out on one side, or the corners might be notched to receive trees, with an outward bow between.*

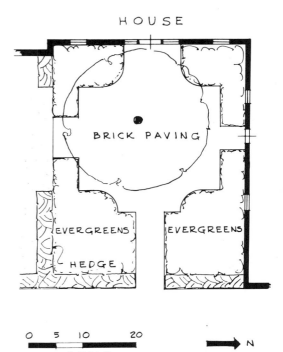

HOUSE

BRICK PAVING

EVERGREENS   EVERGREENS

HEDGE

0   5   10   20
SCALE

N

67 (left). *Most houses are formal
with straight lines and definite angles.
A gracefully curved terrace makes it
more intimate and informal.*

68 (above). *This brick terrace is
located in an angle of the house. It is
basically square with rounded corners
to accommodate bays of low
evergreens and a central tree which
provides adequate shade but does not
interfere with traffic or views.*

103

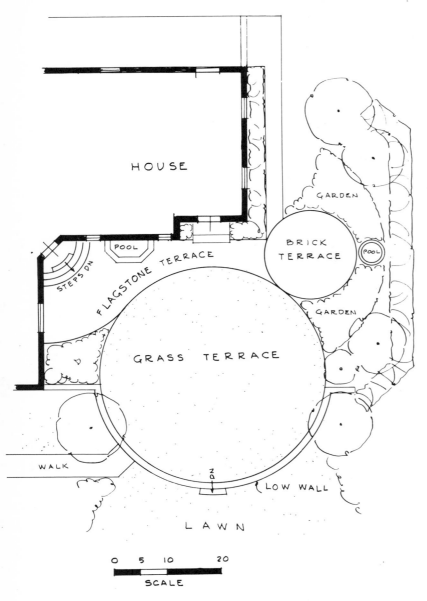

HOUSE

GARDEN

BRICK
TERRACE

POOL

POOL

STEPS DN

FLAGSTONE TERRACE

GRASS TERRACE

GARDEN

WALK

DN

LOW WALL

LAWN

0 5 10 20

SCALE

69. *Three circles are repeated in varying sizes in this garden. A small pool is related to the larger brick terrace in turn related to a large circular grass terrace raised slightly above the general lawn grade. These circular elements are unified by a freeform flagstone terrace edged in brick.*

70. *A circular terrace has a cheerful quality—it's fun. Here the fencing and bed carry the same line, restful to the eye and harmonious. (See photograph 76.)*

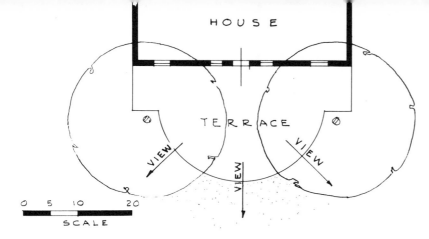

71. *An inadequately narrow rectangular terrace shaded by two large trees was made more usable by adding a semicircular extension at the same level. The curving edge allows for an easy outward flow of both visual and physical activity.*

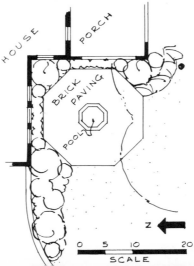

72 and 73 (above and left). *If you can get beyond the intriguing horticultural interests shown here, you will realize that the terrace is an octagon, interesting in itself. (The object in the box in the foreground is a turtle head-on trained on a form with a ficus vine.) The terrace is tucked into a protected corner, decorated with evergreens and shaded by a pair of flowering trees.*

105

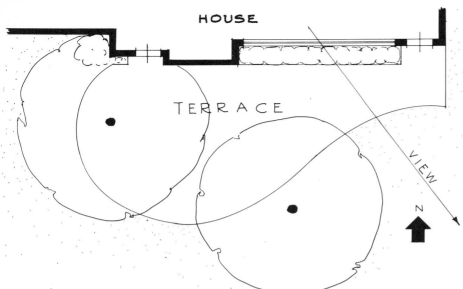

HOUSE

TERRACE

VIEW

N

74. *A spiral form was used for this terrace to make the best use of the view from the living room. On a rectangular terrace the view line would be hung up on a corner; here it slips easily over the flowing edge. Two existing trees were ideally located for afternoon shade, hence the widest part of the terrace is related to the shade pattern.*

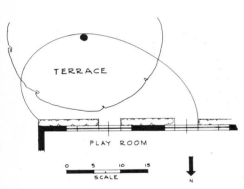

TERRACE

PLAY ROOM

0 5 10 15
SCALE

N

75. *This free-form terrace is paved with bricks laid in sand and edged with a border of brick on end. It provides all-weather sitting on a larger grass terrace at the same elevation. The trunk of a tall black locust is included in the paving; it provides welcome shade. Narrow planting beds separate terrace from the playroom.*

76 (right). *Terrace materials vary considerably, but with traffic going directly in and out of the house an all-weather level surface is particularly important.*

106

77. Brick is one of the most pleasing
and satisfactory surfaces if properly
laid. In large areas, to avoid monotony,
a design in the brickwork adds great
interest and elegance. In time, moss
will fill in around the brickwork; the
trees, shrubs and vines will grow and
the terrace gain even more charm
with maturity.

78. Although it is tricky work,
combining terrace materials can be
intriguing.

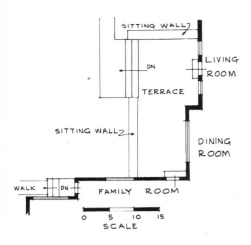

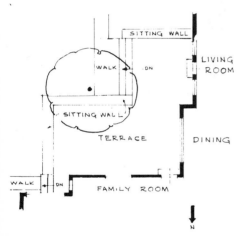

79 and 80 (above). *An existing terrace approximately 10 feet wide was inadequate for family use. It was enlarged by removing one section of wall and adding two new walls to enclose an additional area of 225 square feet on the south side of the family room. A sizeable tree provides noonday and early afternoon shade.*

81 (above right). *A flower bed built into the terrace gives an opportunity for easy color with little work. And plants can be changed with the seasons. Here white and pink petunias will be changed to chrysanthemums in the fall. (See drawing 83.)*

82 (right). *A paved terrace shaded by a pair of trees is bowed outward to improve the proportion and to give a feeling of extension into the lawn and the view beyond; note how it repeats the curve of the bay window to the left.*

83 (far right). *A small narrow concrete paved area was redesigned, raised, enlarged and paved with random rectangular bluestone. It is supported by low fieldstone walls on three sides with built-in beds for the flowers.*

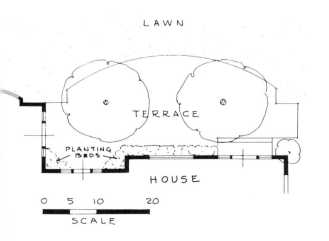

LAWN

TERRACE

PLANTING
BEDS

HOUSE

0 5 10   20
SCALE

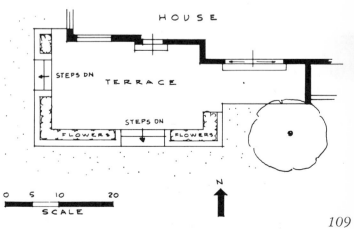

HOUSE

STEPS DN

TERRACE

STEPS DN

FLOWERS   FLOWERS

0 5 10   20
SCALE

N

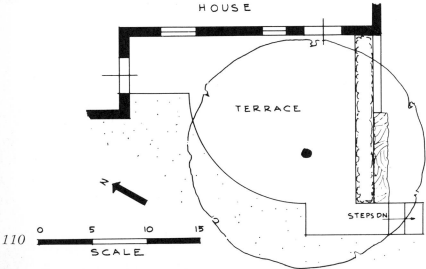

HOUSE

TERRACE

STEPS DN

N

0   5   10   15

SCALE

110

83. *Raised terraces need some enclosure to prevent mishaps. Here a sitting wall serves the purpose admirably.*

84. *Two narrow paved areas at right angles to each other were transformed into an adequate terrace by joining them with a pie-shaped addition which included an old apple tree. There is now room for both circulation and sitting. Such a curved form seems comfortable in a corner space.*

85. *A vine-covered trellis not only gives shade but acts as a radiant cooling system.*

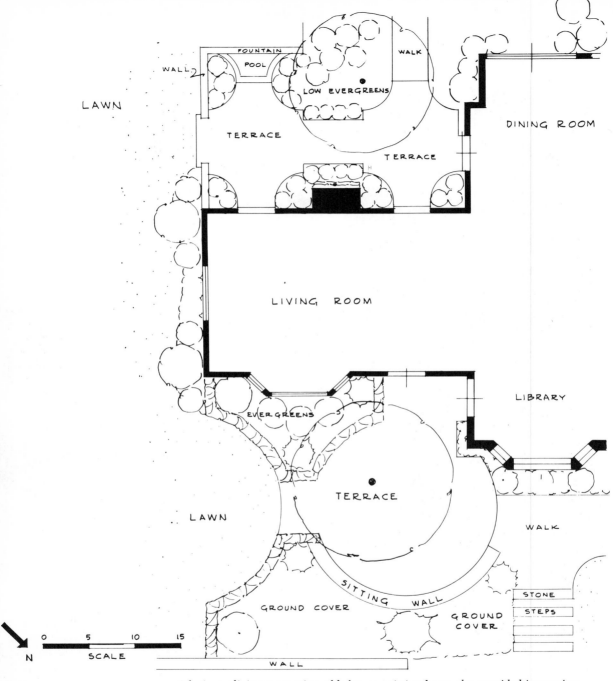

LAWN

FOUNTAIN
POOL

WALL

WALL

TERRACE

LOW EVERGREENS

WALK

DINING ROOM

TERRACE

LIVING ROOM

EVERGREENS

LIBRARY

TERRACE

LAWN

WALK

SITTING WALL

STONE
STEPS

GROUND COVER

GROUND
COVER

0 5 10 15

SCALE

N

WALL

86. *A new living room wing added to an existing house also provided interesting outdoor sitting and garden spaces. A circular terrace of bluestone, accessible from both living room and library, is shaded by a callery pear tree. The circular theme is reflected in sitting wall and evergreen edging which also encloses two beds of low evergreens and ground cover. (See photograph opposite.)*

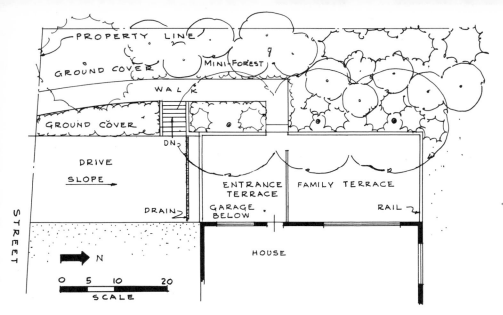

87. *This contemporary house on a narrow suburban lot had a privacy problem. The garage is at basement level; the roof serves as terrace space at first floor level. The main entrance is separated from the family terrace by a wooden louvred partition. A west-facing slope 20 feet wide separates the terrace from the next-door neighbor. Since both afternoon shade and screening were needed, three honey locusts were used to provide light shade and canopy. The remaining space was turned into a mini-forest of yew, gray birch, hemlock and dogwood to provide complete privacy for the terrace.*

88 (below). *The right-sized tree must be selected with a straight clean trunk. It should be placed to the side of a window so that a vista is not obscured.*

7

LAWNS

The English private park with its great sweep of green turf and magnificent specimen shade trees once set the standard for lawns. Today even large places have reduced the size of mowed lawns to relatively limited areas near the house. Even though the lawn is a maintenance problem, it should not be eliminated completely as nothing can quite take its place; no paving or ground cover is quite as satisfactory for walking, sitting, playing or lying on as good green grass.

The lawn is man's version of nature's open space: the prairie, the field, the meadow, the woodland opening. The simple uncluttered lawn gives a feeling of restfulness and repose, providing an opportunity for the mind to ponder, to escape.

A well-designed lawn, enframed or enclosed, is a garden in itself. Like other elements in the landscape, the lawn needs a definite form— the smaller the space, the greater the need for a strong simple contour. A small lawn with a fussy shape or wiggly edges would be restless and distracting. One attractive solution is to treat the lawn as a grass panel with a neat crisp form: a rectangle, circle, octagon, square or oval. The terrace and house may form one side or end of this lawn panel, with beds of flowers and/or ground cover and shrubs forming the remaining sides. The effect can be formal or informal, as desired.

The oval or elliptical lawn or grass panel is an attractive landscape form. The encircling line is simple and flowing; the planted shapes carved out on both sides of the boundary can be visually rewarding. Furthermore it fits nicely into the rectangular space so often a part of residential land subdivision.

The golden mean ratio (as described on page 90) can also be a guide to good proportions in the ellipse or oval. Gardeners with an artistic eye may not need a guideline; others, including the author, find that it has many useful applications when working with outdoor space. Drawing 93 illustrates a small garden with a terrace and an oval lawn. The golden mean was used in choosing the proportions of the terrace and the oval and to create the pleasant relationship between *115* them. The terrace is a rectangle 20 feet long and 12 feet wide. The terrace length (20 feet), is used to establish an attractive width for the oval lawn—32 feet. Next we use the golden mean to find the proper length for the 32-foot oval. The answer is approximately 52 feet. Of course this ratio is used only as a guide; one can stake out an oval on the ground, using a hose or a quantity of 8 by 7/8-inch wooden plant labels, adjusting them until the form enclosed seems attractive from every point of view.

The enclosing line of the oval can be delineated by a stepping-stone path laid on sand with grass joints. Stones should be at least 18 inches square spaced 2 feet from center to center, with the inner edges of the stones following the line of the ellipse. If flat fieldstones are used, the neatest edge should form the line of the lawn panel. Outside the ellipse, beds of ground cover and/or flowers can form the foreground; further back in the bed, so as not to overhang the path, a border or bed of flowering shrubs and/or evergreens will frame and enclose the garden. On a small property, this may represent the entire outdoor living space. On a larger place, it might be a single garden room off the breakfast terrace.

Drawing 94 shows the same grass ellipse in more formal attire. A hedge, wall or fence may enclose the space with corner accents of flowering trees or specimen evergreens. The lawn should be neatly outlined with a low tidy edging plant, clipped or unclipped and preferably evergreen so that it is attractive even in the snow. It is important to install a mowing strip between the lawn and edging plants to eliminate hand edging and aching backs, and to maintain the neat form of the grass oval. (See Chapter 18.) Planting beds may then be used as desired. They can be green gardens of ground covers and groups of small-and medium-sized broadleaved evergreens with larger ones here and there for emphasis or screening. If this is the only garden area, part of the sunny beds can be used for flowers.

The neat oval lawn with its carefully defined edge is not appro-

priate for every place. An informal setting may call for a relaxed flowing line to separate a more casual oval of mowed grass and ground
cover or enclosing shrubs. This line requires skill and sensitivity because
informal lines and spaces are more difficult to design than basic formal
ones with established proportions.

Fortunate indeed are people whose outlook is extended by a view.
Many who own a 50 by 100-foot bit of earth enjoy vistas which they
neither maintain nor pay taxes to support. A view needs a frame to set
it off. Distractions and unattractive features should be screened out and
plants are the most useful materials for this. The tree that shades the
terrace may also frame the view. The dominant plants in the shrub
border may frame and screen at the same time.

The informal oval is also a satisfactory form for the large lawn
or meadow, and the larger the area the more casual its edges may be.
Here the neat boundary gives way to a soft fluid line of bays and in-
dentations with bolder groups of boundary shrubs forming promen-
tories along the grassy edges. However, it is important to maintain a
pleasant proportion between the main open space and the sizes and
shapes of smaller bays at the sides. Sometimes only the nearby portion
of a large lawn or meadow is mowed. In this case the portion nearest
the house can be shaped into the beginnings of an oval, partially
framed. Occasionally, a small amount of lawn adjacent to the house is
mowed regularly, while the area beyond is treated as a meadow with
only one or two mowings each year. Sometimes the mowed lawn with
the house at its center is a square, carved out of the grass. A more
pleasant line is one that curves outward into the meadow, in response
to sight-lines from the house or from other areas overlooking the
meadow.

A hard straight line dividing the view is far more frustrating to
the eye than a long circular curve with the viewer somewhere near the
center of the imaginary circle. This problem is more easily solved if
there is a change of grade between the nearby lawn and the meadow.

Sometimes it is only necessary to mow beyond the crest of the slope and let the meadow begin. Or use a low retaining wall, invisible from the house; mow out to the top of the wall and let the meadow carry on below.

Trees used singly or in small groups add interest to open spaces. As in a painting they contribute greatly to the feeling of foreground, middle and background, especially if the land is relatively level. A very small lawn has room for only one tree, but it can perform several functions by shading the terrace, casting shadow lace across the lawn and framing the garden picture. Larger areas can use carefully placed freestanding trees, or even groups of trees to add interest to the composition without destroying the open feeling. Landscape paintings give suggestions on how to do this. Groups of trees on a lawn serve another purpose, too. One clump may catch the sunlight and leap into prominence to make a delightful center of interest, only to be subordinated by shadow. Another group may be lighted to create another center of interest, producing a different picture. These groups stand out, adding interest against a quieter backdrop.

Shadows play a very important part in the enjoyment of grass areas. A bare sunlit lawn is glaring and uninteresting in the midday sun. The pattern of shadows which shift as the hours pass makes the scene more alive. However, it is better to keep more area in sun than in shade. The long shadows of late afternoon add the most interest; plan the shadow effects for this time of day when people relax and enjoy them. Just as a flight of steps is more interesting when shadow patterns fall upon it, so is a lawn with long shadows reaching across, revealing the delicate gradations in its surface.

The grading and drainage of outdoor areas is covered in Chapter 13, but a few suggestions on the refinement of lawn surfaces are included here. A lawn of any size is often improved by a bit of surface modeling; minor changes can sometimes be made with shovel and wheelbarrow. A lawn should never be entirely flat; tilt or pitch it

89. *A simple, uncluttered lawn, regardless of size, gives a feeling of restfulness and repose. No plant material, esthetically or practically, can quite take the place of good green grass.*

90. *Our English heritage is responsible for the lawn. Most of our large estates with spacious lawns are broken up, but now and then a beautiful sweep of lawn remains.*

slightly so that water flows away from the house. The most interesting lawn is slightly saucer-shaped; it is the perfect form for a small lawn since every square inch will be visible to the eye. In poorly-drained areas where water may stand in the center, the saucer shape may be kept intact but the whole saucer should be tilted slightly away from the house or to the side to allow for drainage.

A gradual upslope gives the greatest amount of visible space and adds to the apparent size of the area. The least interesting lawn surface is the dome shape because at least half of it is hidden from view. A long view downhill may be easy and gradual but a sudden drop in grade limits the amount of visible surface. In that case the lawn profile becomes an important line, forming the base of the picture. A lawn that drops off quickly should be mowed over the crest so as to present a clean neat edge over which the eye moves easily to the view beyond.

Although grass requires continual care, it is still the most pleasant and most easily maintained form of ground cover. Various substitutes have been suggested as alternatives. One can live with green concrete but how unattractive, and even concrete needs to be swept occasionally. Other ground covers serve many needs, but they can never completely take the place of grass. Most popular are the evergreen varieties, such as myrtle, pachysandra and English ivy, which add a slight elevation, color, texture and provide year-round interest. Where intermittent shade exists they may be used in place of lawn; in most homes they are used in addition, often as a transition between lawn and shrubs or evergreens. They make a rich green edging around the base of buildings where mowing would be difficult, and they also reduce heat, noise, dust and glare. They may be used as design elements: ground covers make stylish patterns of green in paved areas, breaking up large expanses. Elsewhere they may take the place of the herbaceous border.

Use paving, lawn and cultivated beds where they are needed, but narrow strips, tight spots or sloping parts of the lawn should be turned into beds of ground cover. Banks and slopes can be clothed with

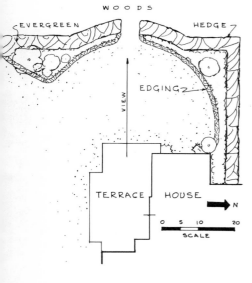

91. The view from the end of this terrace and living room originally looked into a clipped hemlock hedge which separated lawn from woods. A more interesting and longer view was created by making an opening in the hedge and relocating several hemlocks to form a curved hedgeline centered on the view. Low evergreen edging gives crisp form to the lawn and sets off beds at the base of the hedge.

92. *A well-designed lawn is a garden in itself. A lawn of elliptical shape with a border of flowers and shrubs is pleasing without being stiff.*

vigorous ground cover plants. Although ground covers are expensive to install and require considerable hand-weeding for the first two years, once established they become a low-maintenance item.

LAWN GAMES

Since a number of games are played on grass areas it is well to consider their space requirements, for a single plant can ruin an otherwise perfect spot for an occasional game. Small spaces can accommodate box hockey, tether tennis and table tennis. Darts, horseshoes, boccie and quoits will fit into a long narrow space. A level stretch of paving can be marked off for shuffleboard, while a basketball backstop can be a temporary fixture in the paved service yard or garage court.

A medium-sized stretch of lawn can be used for badminton (54 feet by 24 feet) or deck tennis (39 feet by 18 feet), plus a bit of additional space at the sides. Wherever possible, courts should be oriented north and south; playing into the afternoon sun is a decided disadvantage. Croquet is good on a 30 feet by 60 feet area but is very adaptable, while volley ball requires a 30 feet by 60 feet rectangle with 10 feet of additional clear space all around. Room for pitch-and-putt golf can usually be found.

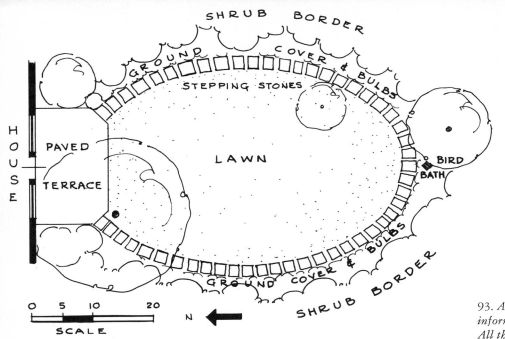

SHRUB BORDER

GROUND COVER & BULBS

STEPPING STONES

HOUSE

PAVED

TERRACE

LAWN

BIRD BATH

GROUND COVER & BULBS

SHRUB BORDER

0 5 10 20

SCALE

N

93. *An oval lawn surrounded by an informal enclosure of plant material. All the proportions are based on the golden mean.*

94. *An oval used as the grass panel in a more formal setting.*

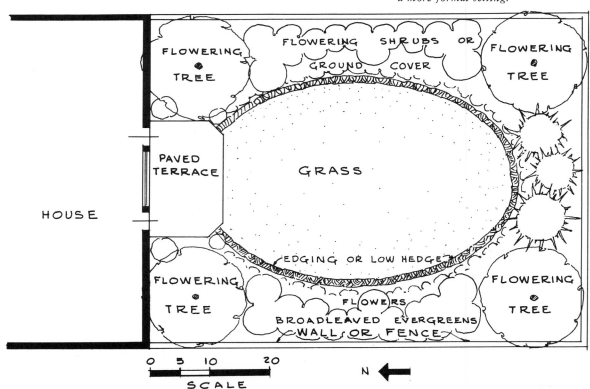

FLOWERING TREE

FLOWERING SHRUBS OR

GROUND COVER

FLOWERING TREE

HOUSE

PAVED TERRACE

GRASS

EDGING OR LOW HEDGE

FLOWERING TREE

FLOWERS

BROADLEAVED EVERGREENS

WALL OR FENCE

FLOWERING TREE

0 5 10 20

SCALE

N

95. *Less formal homes call for a lawn more fluid than definite in shape. As in this case, the proportion of lawn in the overall unity is a sensitive one.*

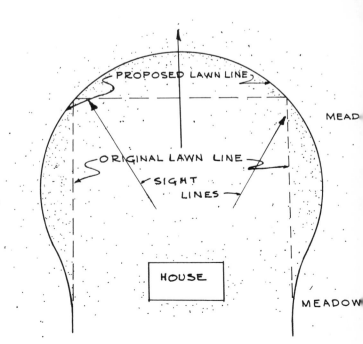

96. *Mowed lawn carved out of a larger meadow is more attractive if the lawn boundary is curved.*

97. *Exurban properties, though building up fast, tend to be more spacious and often run into fields or meadows. A mow line keeps maintenance down and provides a subtle enframement.*

98. (a) *If the lawn slopes away toward the meadow, mow beyond the crest of the slope and leave the tall grass unmowed.*
(b) *A low retaining wall is used to separate lawn and meadow where there is a change of grade.*

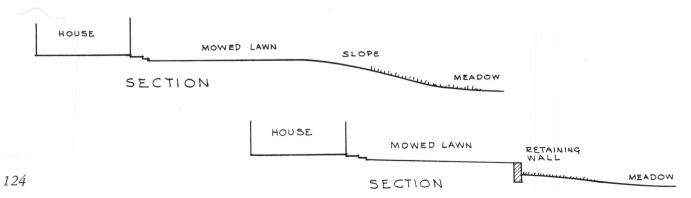

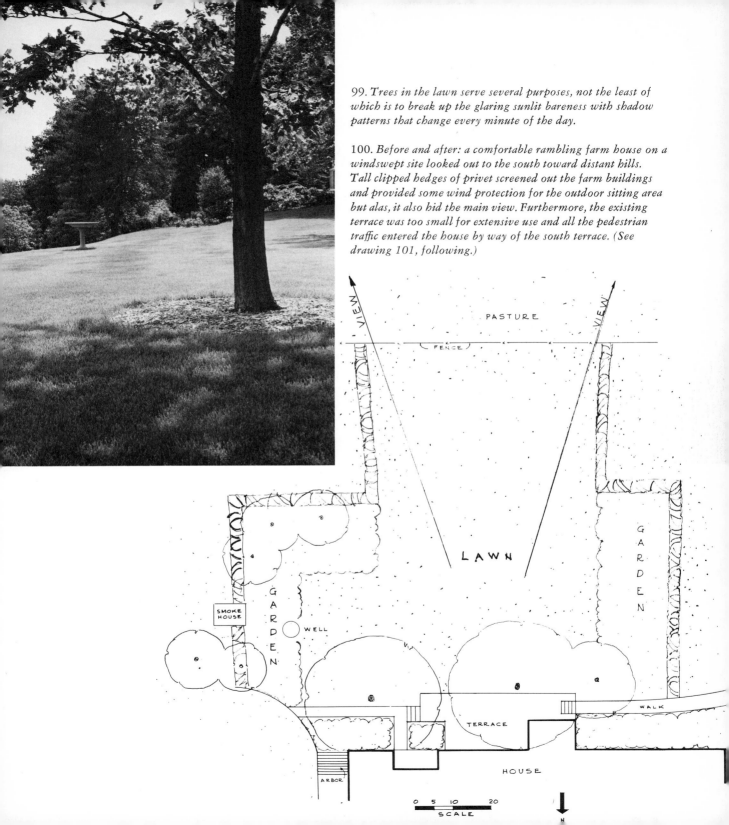

99. *Trees in the lawn serve several purposes, not the least of which is to break up the glaring sunlit bareness with shadow patterns that change every minute of the day.*

100. *Before and after: a comfortable rambling farm house on a windswept site looked out to the south toward distant hills. Tall clipped hedges of privet screened out the farm buildings and provided some wind protection for the outdoor sitting area but alas, it also hid the main view. Furthermore, the existing terrace was too small for extensive use and all the pedestrian traffic entered the house by way of the south terrace. (See drawing 101, following.)*

PASTURE

VIEW

VIEW

(FENCE)

LAWN

GARDEN

GARDEN

SMOKE HOUSE

WELL

WALK

TERRACE

ARBOR

HOUSE

0   5   10   20
SCALE

N

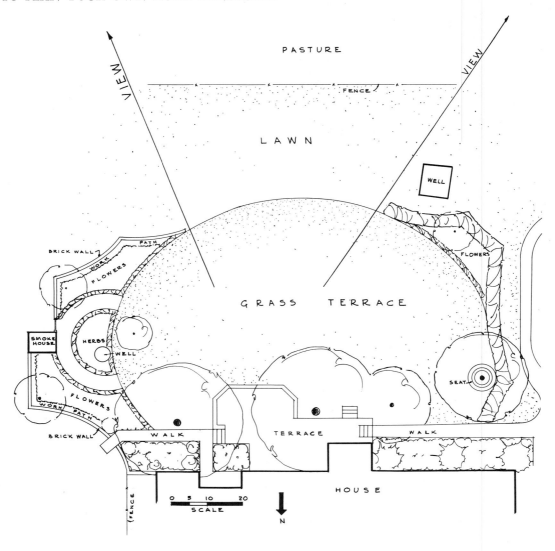

101. *In redesigning the outdoor space an adequate parking area was provided east of the house and an east door and entrance walk became the guest entrance. The brick terrace was enlarged to provide more sitting space. Privet hedges were pulled out, bringing the distant hills into view. The angular lawn area was transformed into a sizeable elliptical grass terrace in good scale with the house; the grade was raised a foot at the south edge of the ellipse to correct the slope and give unity to the oval form. High brick walls were added on the east to separate public and private space and to screen out farm buildings from the terrace. The old smoke house was made the center of an interesting garden. (See Chapter 8.)*

102. *Ground cover can break up an expanse of lawn and give it more form, particularly in a shady area where grass does not grow well.*

8

SWIMMING POOLS

The home swimming pool is a family project that easily outstrips all other recreational features in popularity. Its impact on both the family and the property is sizeable, for pools represent a major investment and occupy considerable space. The installation of a pool should not be a spur-of-the-moment decision made on the first hot day of the season.

Begin by checking zoning regulations, health codes and deed restrictions. Many places require pool plans to be approved by the building inspector. In some backyards it may be physically impossible to install a pool due to lack of space, the location of the septic system or an unsatisfactory soil condition. The disposal of the backwash from the pool filter may be a problem—it cannot go into the sanitary sewer or a nearby stream. A dry well may be required, or it may be dispersed over a proper grass area.

In climates where pools are usable for more than half the year the family may prefer to gear the whole outdoor living space to pool activities. A location near the house makes it easy to supervise children, but it also dominates the family's life and its view. Avoid lining up the living room, terrace and pool in a straight line with the setting sun, since glare will be reflected into the house. In a small backyard the pool house may be eliminated if a portion of the garage or a basement playroom can be adapted for pool storage and toilet facilities.

In colder sections of the country a different approach is needed since the winter landscape should be something other than a covered swimming pool. Here a pool must be planned as one feature in the garden, and not allowed to dictate the design of the entire outdoor living space.

Orientation is most important. Pools in full sun may be used more hours per day for a longer season than those in partial shade. A diving board should be oriented so the diver is not blinded by the setting sun. Protection from cold winds will extend the pool season, and windbreaks of fencing or evergreens may be helpful.

Since the advent of gunite, there is no limit to the variety of 129 shapes that can be used for pools. Rectangular ones provide a maximum of swimming space and can be fitted into almost any place, though curved forms are more interesting in the landscape picture. The design of the terrace and the garden may suggest a unique form for the pool.

Sometimes the pool may be placed to one side of the property without destroying the form of the lawn or diminishing its open quality. A spacious setting is to be preferred, as pool users need open play areas and lounging space in both sun and shade. A level spot with an area of 1,500 to 2,000 square feet along one side of the pool can be used for badminton or croquet, or sunbathing and lounging. The other sides will need a minimum width of 8 to 10 feet.

Paving or decking 3 to 4 feet wide around the pool perimeter makes circulation easy and keeps grass clippings out of the water; 10 to 15 feet is needed at the diving end. Paved sitting areas beside the pool are best at the shallow end to avoid splash, and a pool terrace may be related to a pool house which provides for storage, dressing and refreshment. Paving materials should be skid-proof and non-glaring; they may include brick, concrete, flagstone, slate, tile or redwood. Brushed, color-tinted scored concrete is cool and relatively inexpensive. Paving joints should be as tight as possible and all loose materials which may be blown or carried into the pool should be avoided. An enclosing fence, 4 feet high, which meets the safety requirements may be an attractive feature in the garden, giving privacy while subordinating the pool during the winter season. It can also double as a support for evergreen vines or espaliered fruit trees.

Sometimes the pool can be set at a higher elevation than the house floor and the main living terrace. It is pleasant to see the pool terrace, its activity, gay umbrellas and plants in containers, but quite a different matter to look into a pool all winter long. If grades permit the pool terrace to be set 4 to 5 feet above the house floor level, it can be enjoyed in summer and ignored in winter. An attractive set of steps may lead up to the pool, providing a simple architectural setting; or it can have a casual path fitted with comfortable fieldstone steps up a grassy slope. Other sites may have a perfect spot for the pool at a level lower than the house, with easy steps down from the main terrace. Such changes of grade make it possible for different groups to enjoy the outdoor facilities simultaneously.

If the poolside activities are an important part of the family's summer life, a pool garden can be added. Beds of annuals in a gay color scheme supplement a wide variety of plants in containers. Summer blooming shrubs and flowering trees can be chosen for background, enclosure, screen for the filter, or shade for the terrace as needed, but it is well to remember distance and wind direction so they do not contribute to the litter problem. Fifteen to twenty feet away should be ample except for large shade trees.

Water can be brought in by means of fountains, jets or sprays. In a naturalistic setting, a small waterfall can flow into the pool from a stony basin.

103. *This attractively shaped and planted pool fits well into the overall landscape plan.*

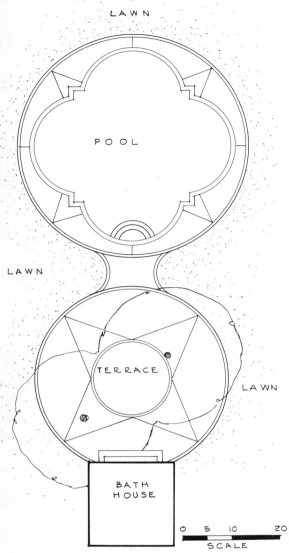

LAWN

POOL

LAWN

LAWN

TERRACE

BATH HOUSE

0 5 10 20
SCALE

104. A quatre-foil pool, 40 feet across, sits on a gentle mound. The circular terrace of brick and bluestone provides shady sitting space beneath a pair of tulip trees and a small existing building was transformed into a charming bath house. (See photograph 107.)

105. Enough paving is needed around the pool to keep grass clippings from getting into it. Here the sunning area and bath house are a contained unit.

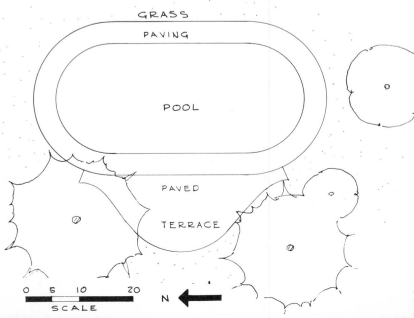

GRASS

PAVING

POOL

PAVED

TERRACE

106 (right). The paved sitting area for this pool is related to the large existing evergreens which provide shade during the hot afternoons.

0 5 10 20
SCALE

N

107. *The elegance of this pool is matched by the unusual intricate pattern of the terrace. This, of course, is not for everyone, but it shows what can be done.*

108. *The oval pool terrace is a combination of cut slope with a low retaining wall supporting the higher land behind it and a level grass terrace on the south side built up with soil from the pool excavation. Paving around the pool perimeter is of scored squares of concrete which also forms the paved terrace between the pool and stone wall. This wall is also used for sitting. The filter/heater is located beyond the shrubbery to the right.*

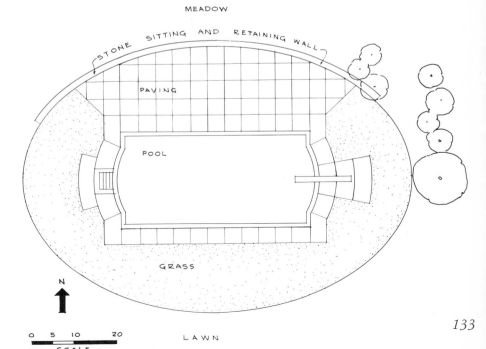

MEADOW

STONE SITTING AND RETAINING WALL

PAVING

POOL

GRASS

N

LAWN

0 5 10   20
SCALE

133

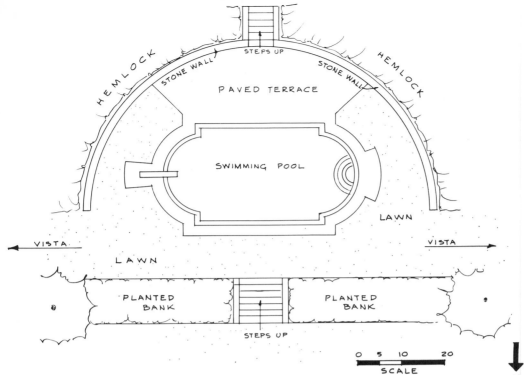

HEMLOCK STONE WALL STEPS UP STONE WALL HEMLOCK

PAVED TERRACE

SWIMMING POOL

LAWN

← VISTA VISTA →

LAWN

PLANTED BANK STEPS UP PLANTED BANK

0 5 10 20
SCALE

N

109. *An open grassy spot at the end of a garden vista and 4 feet above it in elevation made a perfect spot for a swimming pool.*

110. *A pool is not fun to look at in the wintertime. Thus, this pool has been placed above the viewing line from the house—out of sight when not in use.*

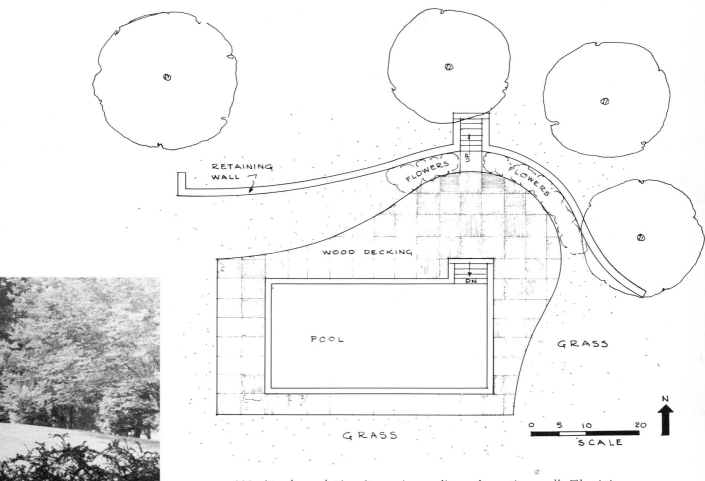

RETAINING WALL

FLOWERS

FLOWERS

UP

WOOD DECKING

DN

POOL

GRASS

GRASS

N

0 5 10 20
SCALE

111. *A pool on a sloping site requires grading and sometimes walls. The sitting area here was cut out of the bank and supported by a fieldstone wall with steps leading to the lawn above. The south side of the pool was made level by using the soil cut out of the bank. A free-form deck is of redwood squares in an alternating pattern; it is separated from the retaining wall by a pool-season garden.*

112. *Colorful planters around pool and sitting area make swimming even more enjoyable here. (See drawing 114.)*

113. *A small pond-shaped pool was located within easy reach of the house and the paved summer terrace which looks out over an informal lawn panel. Placed to the side, it does not detract from the terrace view. A low fieldstone wall absorbs a change of grade and sets off the orchard background.*

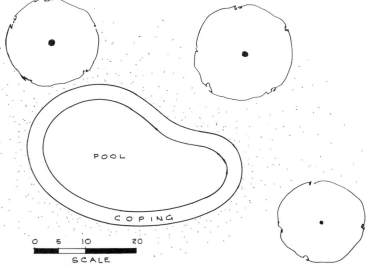

POOL

COPING

0   5   10   20
SCALE

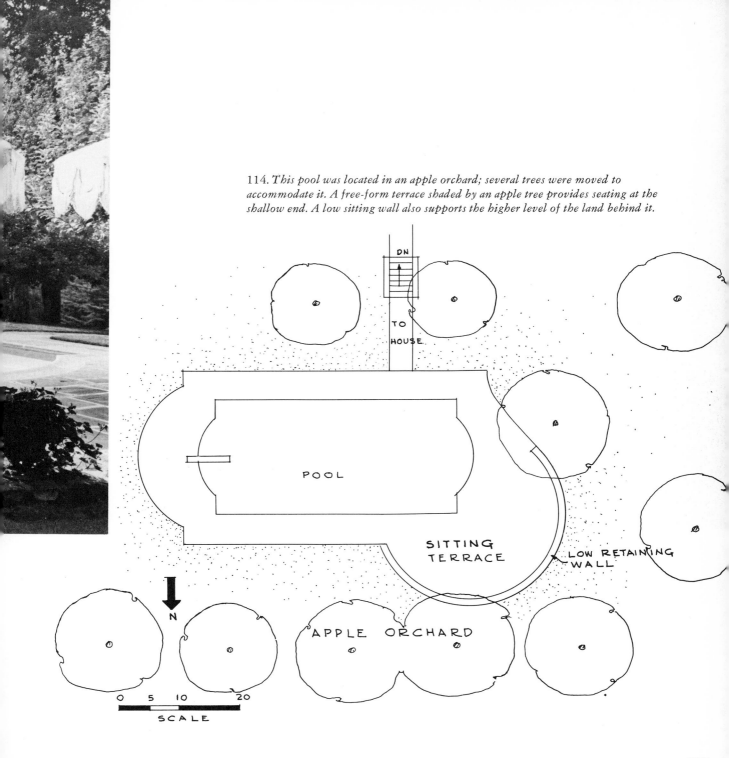

114. *This pool was located in an apple orchard; several trees were moved to accommodate it. A free-form terrace shaded by an apple tree provides seating at the shallow end. A low sitting wall also supports the higher level of the land behind it.*

DN

TO HOUSE

POOL

SITTING TERRACE

LOW RETAINING WALL

N

APPLE ORCHARD

0 5 10 20
SCALE

137

9

GARDENS

Gardening is a form of ancient folk art stretching back in time to the first permanent dwelling; its history is an unfolding story of man and his relationship with land and shelter. Changing continually in form and substance gardens have served a basic human need and will undoubtedly become more important as the quality of our environment declines and the complexities of life increase.

The great era of American estates was during the late 19th and early 20th century. A few remain, reduced in size; some are now institutions, but most have been destroyed and the land subdivided. These great gardens, however, left their imprint. The pattern of the formal flower garden with its main axis centered on a window or door and ending in a terminal feature was scaled down to fit the suburban house and lot. It was a garden to be looked at and strolled through rather than lived in. Many were merely patterns copied from older gardens with no attempt to adapt them to a new location and a new era. This was the formal school of garden planning.

There was also the informal school. It began with a true respect for nature, but developed into a formless, degenerate style with wiggly walks and beds of spotty scattered plants—a travesty on nature. This era bloomed and waned and eventually disappeared.

Fortunately, along with renewed interest in the environment, a simple naturalistic approach to planting has developed. Today's garden is formed around a new concept—an intimate relationship between interior and exterior space with surfaces of paving and grass for sitting, eating, working, playing and gardening, surrounded by plants for shade, interest and enclosure. It is for gardeners and nongardeners.

Such a concept does not exclude cultivated beds of flowers for mass effect, but if they are to be assets rather than liabilities, it is wise to take stock before assuming the initial expense and continuing burden of maintenance they require. Even without gardens most places need some care. It is important to strike a balance between a beautiful flower garden and a small, easy-to-maintain combination of various flowering plants and evergreens. The garden must be in keeping with the family's way of life—a large formal garden is out of place with a casual house and a relaxed style.

It must be remembered that a garden of flowers alone is unattractive for half the year. To produce a feeling of peace and beauty, flowers need a well designed setting, just as a picture needs an appropriate frame. Most of today's gardens are small so that the owners can take care of them, but even small gardens can be visually rewarding. They should have strong simple form and line in beds or borders, with neat edgings and appropriate backgrounds or enclosures. Plants should be chosen for form, color, texture and outline, with some feature—an unusual plant or simple architectural accent—as a focus for the composition.

Today's garden is to look at, to walk through and to live in. Sometimes a combined garden and sitting area is possible; the paved terrace is an open space, with flower beds at each side and lawn in the foreground. In such a garden one can weed from a folding camp stool without missing any of the conversation.

Beside the house or the terrace, or between them, might be a good spot for a small garden. Compact evergreens on each side of the doorway and a few additional evergreens would frame it, while a neat evergreen edging would separate beds from terrace. In a small space these two elements might be enough to provide form and structure in winter. Early flowering shrubs or evergreens and small early bulbs would start the season. (Don't use narcissus; its long foliage season presents a problem.) Tidy spring-blooming perennials plus a few tulips tucked under shrubs or in front of peonies will carry the spring show. Long-flowering annuals are the mainstay for summer. As they become tired in late summer, budding chrysanthemums from pots will carry on the fall picture, and when winter comes, branches of the Christmas tree can cover the bare soil until spring arrives. If there is no room on the terrace for a mini-garden, use plants in containers. There are excellent how-to books complete with lists of plants for container gardening.

Many combinations of small neat gardens and paved terraces are attractive and easily cared for. A garden design may evolve from available space. An angle of the house can be used for a terrace with lawn at one side and a small garden on the other. This gives a closely related and nicely integrated pattern of terrace for sitting, garden for interest and lawn for open space. In a more exposed spot a terrace and garden can be combined and enclosed. The center of one such garden is a circular brick terrace shaded by a honey locust tree. An octagonal garden of flowers and evergreens surround the terrace while steps provide access to the house. The combined garden and terrace is enclosed by a pierced brick wall high enough to shut out the immediate surroundings when one is seated, yet low enough to serve as a base for the view in the distance.

A dooryard can be an ideal spot for a green garden; few gardens are more delightful the year round. They are basically evergreen in framework, with deciduous accents for height and small flowering trees or shrubs for color. The successful green garden, drawing heavily upon broad-leaved evergreens, depends on variety of form and texture. This is a subtle and sophisticated form of outdoor art, highly useful in today's landscape. A green garden need not be lacking in flowers; andromeda, myrtle, azaleas, laurel, skimmia and various rhododendron add a sequence of color. (See Chapter 4, illustrations 30 and 31.)

A small property with a restricted amount of private space is the spot for an outdoor living room. Do not divide the space into lawn, garden and terrace, but have an all-in-one combination. In the small modern house, the living room, dining room and sometimes even the kitchen are closely related with little or no division. Outdoors we apply the same principle. The boundaries constitute the walls and most of its decoration as well, and flowers can be part of this decoration.

On larger places, the location for a garden may grow out of a natural space suggesting the form or appropriate plant material. Existing evergreens with a sunny foreground may indicate a protected spot for a garden. At other times the selection of a site may be purely arbitrary. Sun should be a major consideration; poor soil can be improved but there is no substitute for sun. If there is no view from the house, the garden may be the center of interest set against a neutral background. An intimate enclosed space can be created almost anywhere you like.

If the house is fortunate in having a view, the garden should not upstage it. Few things are more annoying than a garden in front of the view where the eye must continually shift from one to the other. Keep the lawn open as foreground and give the garden separate billing by placing it to one or both sides of the view. A garden may be the main feature or one of several that give pleasure without monopolizing the entire scene.

New gardeners sometimes say "I want a perennial garden so I can have flowers all seasons without any work." Would that it were so! Perennials do require care and it is almost impossible to have a continuous blaze of color with perennials alone. For a long summer season of continuous bloom, annuals provide more flowers per square foot for less effort than perennials. A garden must contain several kinds of flowers if it is to provide maximum bloom for the longest season. It can begin with early bulbs and early-blooming perennials with some tulips and perhaps pansies or similar bedding plants. There may be several kinds of annuals to supplement the summer-blooming perennials, but tired annuals should be replaced with potted ready-to-bloom chrysanthemums that carry color through the autumn and supplement the limited number of fall-blooming perennials.

As the distance from the house increases and year-round visibility becomes less important, gardens may take on more casual and relaxed forms. Even perennials such as daylilies with their many varieties and long blooming season can be used as an informal border between a foreground of lawn and a background of shrubs, wall, fencing or meadow. Separate the grass and the planting bed with a mowing strip of brick and/or metal curbing to keep the flowing line, to eliminate the need for edging, and to keep grass out of the planting bed. The daylily season may be extended by using narcissus in front of them and by adding sizeable clumps of yellow helenium (or similar easy perennials) to lengthen the season of bloom. Such a garden will have no form or mass in winter, but will provide a colorful three-season display.

Perennials need care, but can be grown with a minimum of attention. They are often strung out in a line between shrub border and lawn, a spot with so much competition that it hardly does justice to even the most obliging of perennials. It is much better to group the easy ones together in a sizeable bed at some distance from the house. This prevents holes left by dormant Oriental poppies and dead flower heads from detracting from the overall display of colors. Use five to nine plants of a species together to make a real show when they bloom, rather than the one or two one would set in a smaller, nearby garden.

The amount of bloom seen from the house depends upon the shape of the bed. If one looks into the end of a bed, with the eye traveling from the front to the tallest plants at the rear the impact of color is considerable. In some situations it is possible to have two beds, flanking an informal lawn area. Groups of flowers can be repeated in sequence, since few flower colors clash in nature. If strong hues of pink and orange are desired, they can be used in separate beds with grass between. Flowering shrubs provide background for such beds, but they should be separated by a generous grass path so the shrubs will not hang over the beds nor shade them excessively. It will also keep shrub roots from invading and competing with the perennials. Lilacs have unusually aggressive root systems and should be kept away from all flower beds.

If there is no view, a single bed of easy-maintenance perennials may be placed at the end of the lawn. Drawing 141 shows a crescent-shaped bed backed by a low fieldstone wall which divides the lawn from an apple orchard. Here the eye travels from side to side, flowing easily over the curved line in the foreground. The color density is not as great as that shown in Drawing 139, but roses, perennials, or annuals in beds in the foreground can increase the effect.

Another point is worth bearing in mind: many flowers turn their faces to the sun. Some of the most light-sensitive ones face east in the morning and west in the afternoon, thus flower beds on the north, east or west sides of the property will have more flower faces on display. A protected north garden open to the sun produces a fine display of flowers. Narcissi should be planted north of the spot from which they will be seen.

With the development of easier-to-use insect and disease controls, many gardens can include a small rose bed or a row of favorite roses for cutting. Most roses are not beautiful plants though they bear beautiful flowers. Resist the temptation to put them in beds on the terrace where one must endure their ungainly habit and their less than attractive winter trappings needed for their survival. Give roses a small garden of their own, enclosed by a fence, with walks and working beds narrow enough so that bushes can be reached for pruning, spraying, cutting or hilling up, without the gardener being shredded by thorns. Or use small beds with a neat edging and some kind of background, at the side of the lawn or grass panel. A small rose garden around a pool, sundial or bit of statuary should have a strong neat edging so that the design is visible even without the blossoms.

Wind protection is important for roses in winter. In severe climates a south exposure or the south side of a wall is a good location. Drawing 145 illustrates a small rose garden on the south side of a bedroom wing in which the form grew out of the need for wind protection.

If you enjoy flowers in the house a small cutting garden should be included, since you can't have your flowers and cut them too. In a limited space a combined vegetable and cutting garden is a fine arrangement, since both crops are to be harvested. With the rising cost of food, many families are growing their own vegetables, tilling the earth and bringing forth harvests unsurpassed in freshness and quality. Such gardens can also be attractive. A sizeable plot should be fenced to keep out dogs and rabbits; it is best divided into beds with short rows to encourage a sequence of plantings and harvests. Paths edged with flowers for cutting can be used to divide sections of vegetables. The ideal spot for a vegetable garden is sunny, with good soil and air circulation, located conveniently near the tool shed. It can be screened from the main lawn by an attractive fence or an evergreen hedge which would double as a background for a flower border, enjoyed from the house and terrace. A row of blueberries or dwarf fruit trees, or an attractive grape arbor, can also divide the lawn and vegetable garden.

Raised beds enclosed by wood 2-by-12's or railroad ties also form a neat and useful vegetable garden, which might make a pattern of green in a gravel court. A charming garden of small raised beds can be

115. *Gardens like these were to be looked at and walked through rather than lived in.*

116. *As respect for nature grew, an "informal school" of gardening developed, only to soon wane. It did, however, leave its mark in a free flowing style.*

146

made with square flue tiles set on soil or gravel. Beds surrounded by grass may be edged with brick or railroad ties set flush with the grass so trimming and edging are not a problem. Each bed can hold a separate crop—one for salads, another for herbs, a third for annuals and another for strawberries. Each child might have a garden bed for his own. Consider carefully the amount of space you wish to care for; the enthusiasm of springtime does not always survive the dog days of August. Land once put into cultivation must be maintained, otherwise nature takes over with weeds.

The kinds of gardens are as varied as the gardeners who make them. The gardener's interests and site can suggest a rock garden, wild garden, heather garden, wall garden, bog garden or herb garden. Other gardens feature a favorite flower while some are spring gardens, fall, or even winter gardens. They each serve a need simply by giving pleasure.

117. Gardens today are often simple settings for enjoying life outdoors.

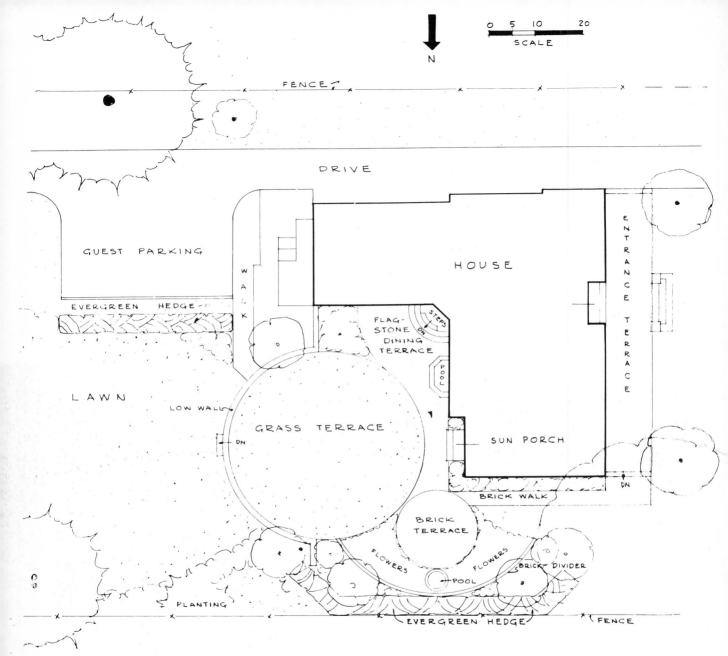

FENCE

N

0 5 10 20
SCALE

DRIVE

GUEST PARKING

EVERGREEN HEDGE

W A L K

HOUSE

ENTRANCE TERRACE

FLAG-STONE DINING TERRACE

STEPS

DN

POOL

LAWN

LOW WALL

GRASS TERRACE

DN

SUN PORCH

BRICK WALK

DN

BRICK TERRACE

FLOWERS

POOL

FLOWERS

BRICK DIVIDER

PLANTING

EVERGREEN HEDGE

FENCE

118. *On this suburban property a combination of brick and flagstone provides alternative sitting areas for different hours of the day. The circular brick terrace is enhanced by a small semicircular garden and pool with a background of azaleas, small flowering trees and an evergreen hedge. A large circular grass terrace, providing intimate lawn area at the same level, was made possible by adding a low retaining wall. The existing oval lawn at a slightly lower level is enclosed by mixed shrubs and evergreens.*

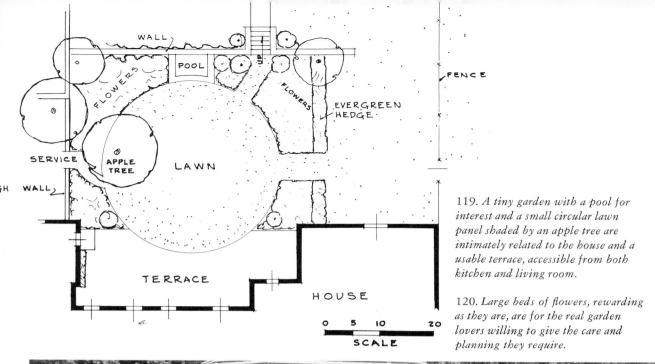

Labels on the plan: WALL, POOL, UP, FLOWERS, FLOWERS, FENCE, EVERGREEN HEDGE, SERVICE, APPLE TREE, LAWN, H WALL, TERRACE, HOUSE

SCALE
0   5   10   20

119. *A tiny garden with a pool for interest and a small circular lawn panel shaded by an apple tree are intimately related to the house and a usable terrace, accessible from both kitchen and living room.*

120. *Large beds of flowers, rewarding as they are, are for the real garden lovers willing to give the care and planning they require.*

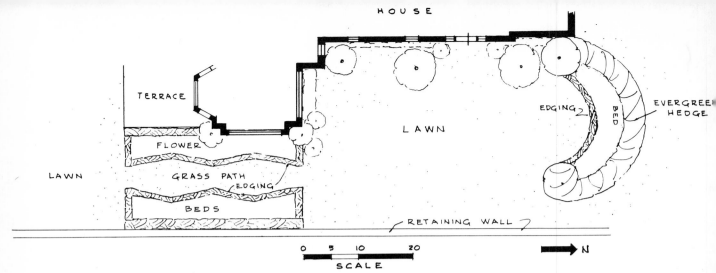

HOUSE

TERRACE

FLOWER

GRASS PATH

EDGING

BEDS

LAWN

LAWN

EDGING BED

EVERGREE HEDGE

RETAINING WALL

0 5 10 20
SCALE

N

121. *Interesting small gardens can be fitted into many odd spaces. Outside the master bedroom an evergreen hedge provides background for a small curved garden bed and insures privacy from the auto court and main entrance. It can be enjoyed from the den as well as the grass terrace off the bedroom. A narrow space between the end of the main terrace and den and a retaining wall was also transformed into a small garden which could be walked through yet enjoyed both from the house and the terrace.*

122. *The space between the main terrace and the small dining terrace is just right for a neat close-at-hand garden featuring a variety of plant material for a four-season effect. (See photograph opposite.)*

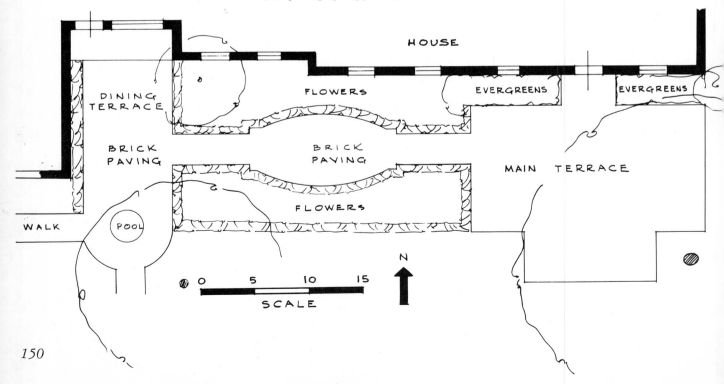

HOUSE

DINING TERRACE

FLOWERS

EVERGREENS

EVERGREENS

BRICK PAVING

BRICK PAVING

MAIN TERRACE

FLOWERS

WALK

POOL

N

0 5 10 15
SCALE

123. *This walk-through garden makes an attractive setting from all points of view. The evergreen edging keeps the form in winter.*

124. *A small garden off an east terrace was inspired by the two small basins from the top of a large Victorian fountain. These were used as the feature in this small pool, surrounded by narrow brick paths setting off corner beds of flowers.*

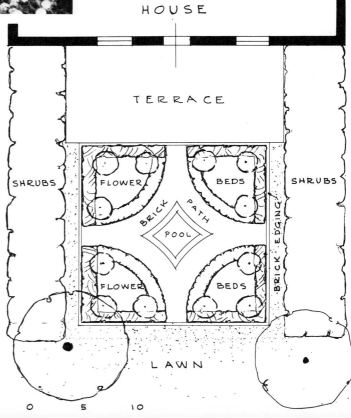

HOUSE

TERRACE

SHRUBS

FLOWER   BEDS

BRICK PATH

POOL

SHRUBS

BRICK EDGING

FLOWER   BEDS

LAWN

0   5   10

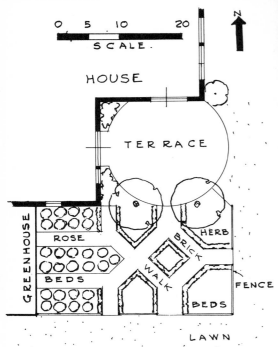

125. *A circular bluestone terrace in a protected angle of the house looks out on the lawn on one hand and a small enclosed herb and rose garden on the other. A pair of callery pear trees provides noonday shade.*

126. *A view of 125. Such small neat gardens and paved terraces are easily cared for.*

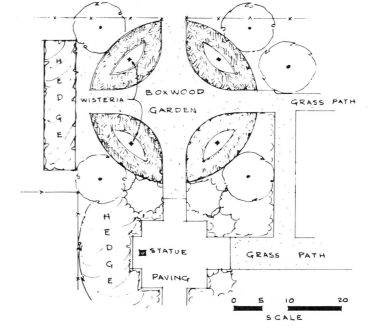

127. *A small unused space was turned into a pattern garden formed of home-propagated boxwood. Height and accent are provided by four wisteria trained on wooden posts about 9 feet high. Two wooden brackets 2½ feet and 2 feet long, extend out from each side of the posts, displaying the wisteria to good advantage.*

128. *Here a terrace and garden are combined. Flowering shrubs and clematis behind the border of boxwood give a succession of bloom. (See drawing below.)*

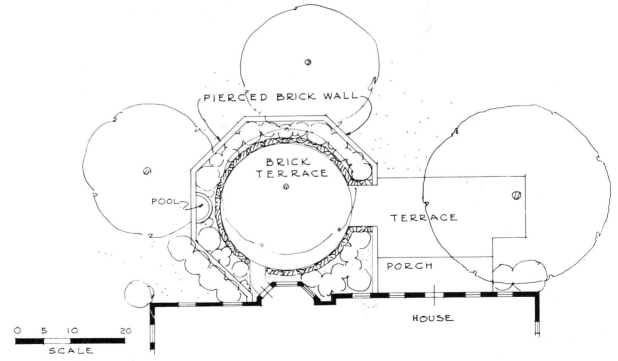

PIERCED BRICK WALL

BRICK
TERRACE

POOL

TERRACE

PORCH

HOUSE

0 5 10 20
SCALE

N

129. *In this plan we see the house with its attached octagonal garden for intimate use, located off the dining room. It is enclosed by a brick wall 4 feet high. Each corner is of solid brick but the panels are of pierced brick construction which permits air circulation and prevents a feeling of claustrophobia.*

153

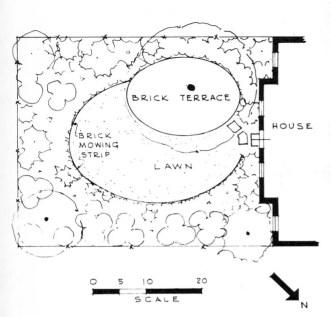

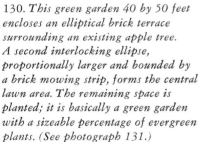

130. *This green garden 40 by 50 feet encloses an elliptical brick terrace surrounding an existing apple tree. A second interlocking ellipse, proportionally larger and bounded by a brick mowing strip, forms the central lawn area. The remaining space is planted; it is basically a green garden with a sizeable percentage of evergreen plants. (See photograph 131.)*

131. *We see how this limited space neatly combines lawn, garden and terrace all in one.*

132 (right). *An unused grass terrace supported by a low retaining wall was transformed into a small garden. A background for flowers was provided by installing a pierced brick wall, using the existing wall as a base. Two beds, each with a curved evergreen edging, add color and interest on each side of the path.*

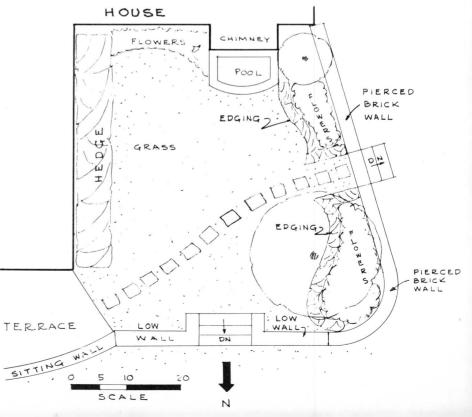

154

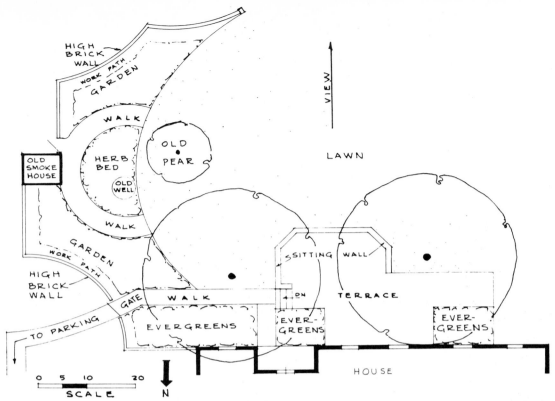

HIGH BRICK WALL
WORK PATH
GARDEN
WALK
OLD SMOKE HOUSE
HERB BED
OLD WELL
OLD PEAR
WALK
GARDEN
WORK PATH
HIGH BRICK WALL
TO PARKING
GATE
WALK
EVERGREENS
EVER-GREENS
VIEW
LAWN
SITTING WALL
ON
TERRACE
EVER-GREENS
HOUSE

0 5 10   20
SCALE
N

133. *A charming old brick smoke house and an old well formed the nucleus of a garden with low herbs in the center foreground; a semicircular brick walk separates the garden into three beds and provides access to larger beds of perennials displayed against a background of high brick walls which screen out the parking area on one hand and farm buildings on the other. The original brick terrace on the south side, too long and narrow to be usable, was extended into the lawn and bordered by a low wall to increase the sitting space.*

134. *Designs may grow out of a natural space area which would determine the shape of the garden. This sunny spot was just right for herbs.*

155

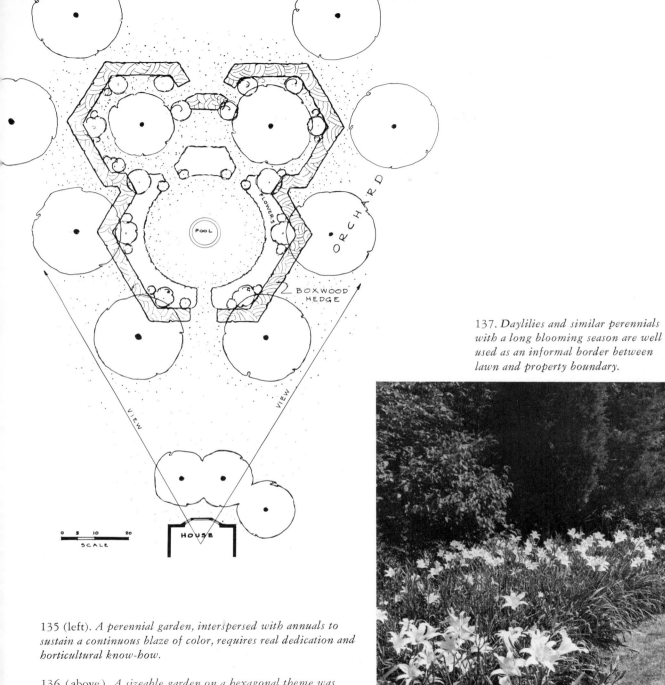

137. *Daylilies and similar perennials
with a long blooming season are well
used as an informal border between
lawn and property boundary.*

135 (left). *A perennial garden, interspersed with annuals to
sustain a continuous blaze of color, requires real dedication and
horticultural know-how.*

136 (above). *A sizeable garden on a hexagonal theme was
inspired by the spacious library at the end of the house. The two
side windows set at 30 degree angles look down allées of fruit
trees to views beyond. The central window with no view
suggested the center line for the garden repeating the 30 degree
angles, hence the hexagonal design.*

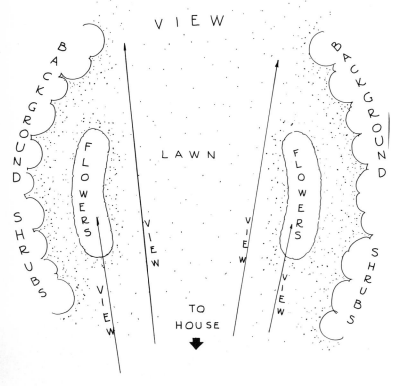

138. *If there is a view do not place flower beds where they must compete with it. Beds may be placed to one or both sides of the lawn and in front of a shrub background but separated from it by a mowed grass path, 4 to 5 feet wide. Here they can be enjoyed in their own right.*

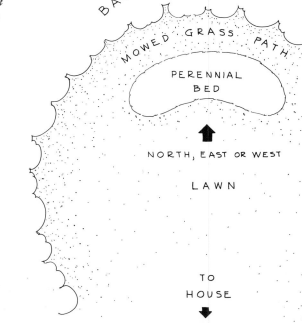

139. *If there is no view, a casual flower bed may be the prima donna, set against a background of shrubs or evergreens but separated from it by a mowed grass path, 4 to 5 feet wide.*

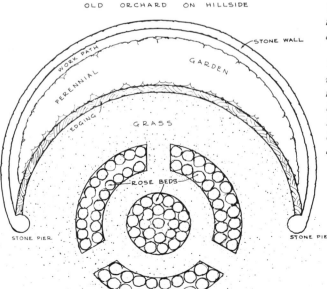

OLD   ORCHARD   ON   HILLSIDE

STONE WALL

WORK PATH

GARDEN

PERENNIAL

EDGING

GRASS

ROSE BEDS

STONE PIER

STONE PIER

0   5   10   15   20
SCALE

140. *Rose bushes are not handsome as plants—it's the bloom that counts. Here an informal rose bed sets them off to advantage.*

141. *In an old orchard on a New England hillside, a fieldstone retaining wall, highest at the center and sloping downward toward the front, serves as background for a sizeable perennial bed. A pair of stone piers 18 inches high terminate the wall. Roses, which do best in separate quarters, are used in circular beds in the center. Bulbs and annuals might be substituted according to personal preference.*

159

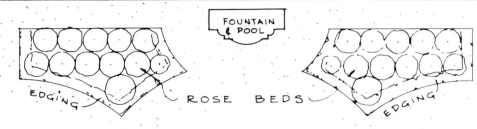

FIELD STONE WALL

FOUNTAIN & POOL

EDGING

ROSE BEDS

EDGING

142. *Two small beds form this tiny rose garden featuring a delightful pool and fountain set against a New England stone wall.*

0   5   10

SCALE

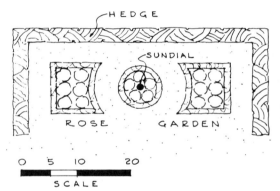

HEDGE

SUNDIAL

ROSE   GARDEN

0   5   10   20

SCALE

143 and 144 (above and right).
Three small rose beds edged with miniature boxwood are set against a background of clipped yew. Roses are best planted by themselves. A formal setting shows them off and gives the garden interest when they are not blooming.

160

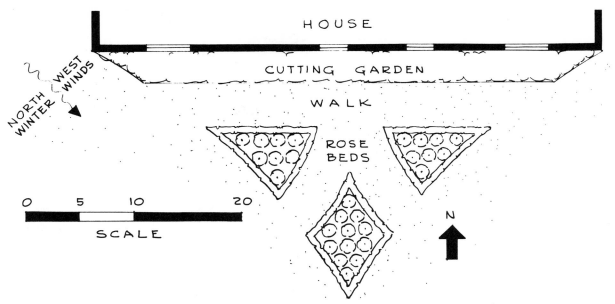

HOUSE

CUTTING GARDEN

WALK

NORTH WEST WINTER WINDS

ROSE BEDS

N

0   5   10   20

SCALE

145. *Three small rose beds are placed at the south end of the house, off the guest and master bedrooms, where they will receive full sun and some protection from winter winds. Furthermore, they will not compete with the important view to the west.*

146. *Most cutting gardens are unattractive except when full of bloom. These gardens are given form and structure and are interesting even when there are no flowers. The beds are divided and space made accessible by wood-chip paths edged with a curb of bricks on end. The center is emphasized by a vine trained on a support, while tree peonies mark the corners. A variety of flowering plants are grown and the effect is different and interesting at all seasons. Vegetables might be interplanted with flowers if desired.*

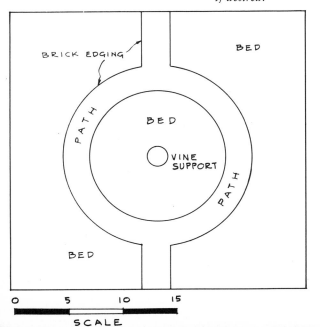

BRICK EDGING

BED

PATH

BED

VINE SUPPORT

PATH

BED

0   5   10   15

SCALE

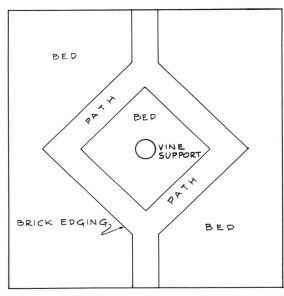

BED

PATH

BED

VINE SUPPORT

PATH

BRICK EDGING

BED

161

147 (right). *Here is a vegetable garden with real style. Right outside of the kitchen door, two currant bushes (trained as standards) mark the entry to the vegetable garden path.*

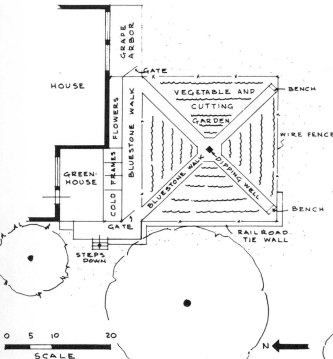

149 (below). *This compact flower, vegetable and fruit garden is utilitarian but not unattractive. Vegetables are grown inside the fenced portion, equipped with an electric wire to discourage raccoons. The 40 by 55 foot area is divided into four beds with a maximum width of 17 feet, which makes for short rows and a sequence of plantings. Paths are of earth bordered by annuals for cutting. A grape arbor separates the garden from tool storage, service yard, and the compost bin. Perennial beds face the open lawn, with the fence as background. A brick mowing strip divides the perennial edging from the lawn. Beds of raspberries, asparagus, strawberries and rhubarb are outside the fence line. (See photograph 150.)*

148. *A sunny spot beside a small house was developed as a 25 by 28 foot vegetable garden. The west slope is supported by a railroad tie wall and the garden is fenced to keep out animals. Neat flagstone walks divide it into four triangular beds; a dipping well in the center serves as a functional feature. In front of the greenhouse is a protected spot for the cold frames and a grape arbor shades the bedroom windows from the summer sun.*

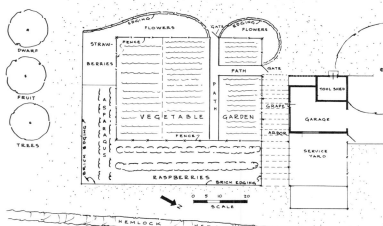

150. *This informal vegetable garden is large enough to give the family fresh vegetables all summer with enough extra to freeze for winter.*

151 (below). *The plan gives this garden a vista from the house through clipped linden trees into a lawn area bordered by flowers, with vegetables, strawberries and asparagus behind.*

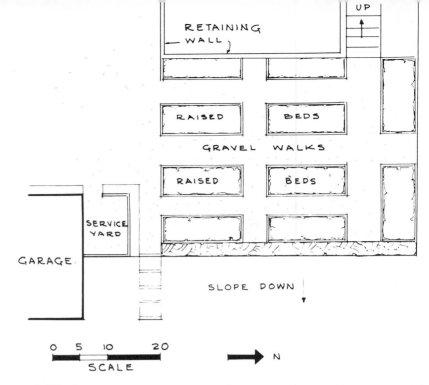

152 and 153 (right and below). *An easy-to-care-for garden designed by a retired architect consists of raised planting beds, 6 by 12 feet in size, built of 2 by 12 inch lumber set on a gravel base adjacent to the garage court. Each bed is devoted to a separate crop—herbs, strawberries, vegetables, annuals, perennials and roses.*

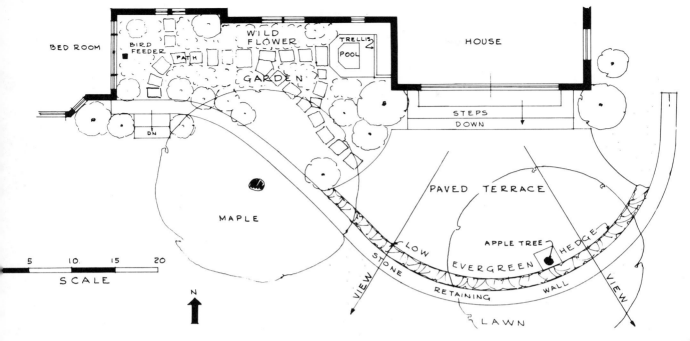

BED ROOM

BIRD
FEEDER

PATH

WILD
FLOWER

GARDEN

TRELLIS

POOL

HOUSE

STEPS

DOWN

DN

PAVED TERRACE

MAPLE

APPLE TREE

HEDGE

LOW

VIEW

EVERGREEN

WALL

STONE

RETAINING

VIEW

5   10.   15   20

SCALE

LAWN

N

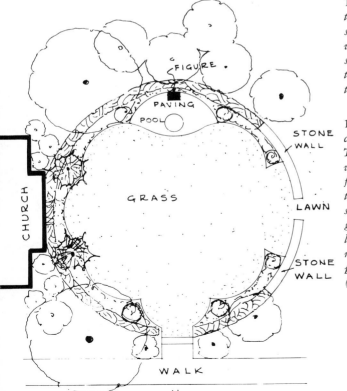

FIGURE

PAVING

POOL

STONE
WALL

CHURCH

GRASS

LAWN

STONE
WALL

WALK

5   10   20

SCALE

N

154. *A stone retaining wall makes possible a level area for a terrace and small wildflower garden on an otherwise steep slope south of this cottage. Steps in front of the sliding glass doors are wide enough to sit on. The view from the bedroom includes a small pool backed by a vine-covered trellis which add interest to an otherwise bare wall. Stepping-stones provide a path through the wild garden.*

155. *Off the fieldstone reredos wall of a small church is a simple circular garden known as the Memorial Garden of Saint Francis. The round form, symbolizing eternity, is enclosed by yew hedge, with background planting, and low fieldstone walls. The bronze figure of Saint Francis with a birdbath at his feet are features of the small stone terrace. A neat edging laid in circular curves separates the center grass panel from small beds of flowers and ground cover, accented by a few flowering shrubs and broad-leaved evergreens. Two hollies mark the corners of the outside reredos wall on which is mounted a plaque with bronze name-plates of those whose ashes are buried in the garden. (See photograph 156, following.)*

165

156. *St. Francis sets the mood for this simple, serene setting.*

10

ENCLOSURE AND CANOPY

If we think of lawn and paving as the floor of our landscape, then enclosure by the sides or walls, and a canopy adding at least a partial ceiling effect, give substance to the three dimensions of length, width, and height. This applies to small garden spaces as well as to an entire property. Enclosures need not be walls in the literal sense, but there should be at least a suggestion of boundary to give a sense of unity. Enclosure may also be decorative as well—a simple picket fence doubling as a clematis bower.

Low barriers are a psychological boundary limiting movement but not vision. Enclosures of medium height may block some movement and vision, but those over 6 feet high are substantial barriers in every way. Materials and methods of enclosure are many and varied—they may be solid, translucent, transparent or pierced. Common enclosures are fencing or panels of wood, wire, plastic, glass or treillage; masonry of brick, stone, concrete block; and plants in various forms and combinations.

The height, width and substance of the enclosure should be in proportion to the space involved. Planting is the least expensive material but it often uses a lot of space. Clipped hedges may be as narrow as 12 inches but require regular shearing. Unclipped hedgerows are less demanding but more widespreading, and an attractive border planting of shrubs and flowering trees requires even more space.

If space is minimal and privacy important, a solid fence 6 to 8 inches thick is the best investment. Height will depend upon need. A 5-foot fence may not be an adequate screen yet be high enough to produce hurt feelings. In some situations a reasonably high fence can be combined with an attractive arbor and overhead vines to screen a difficult spot. Fences or walls on slopes may present problems. If next to a building, they should be level on top or be built in a series of level panels which step up or down with the grade. If the slope is no steeper than 5 per cent, freestanding fences or walls may slope with *167* the grade; otherwise they are best constructed in level panels or subordinated by planting.

Enclosure may be used to define a view, to limit movement, and to temper wind and noise. In our crowded lives, some measure of enclosure is important for a sense of privacy and protection. On hillside lots enclosure is needed primarily to center the view, or provide privacy on the remaining sides. Flat sites without views require complete enclosure if privacy is desired. Where space limitations require walls or fencing, plants are often added to relieve monotony.

The majority of private places rely on plants for most screening. While a garden bed may call for a uniform background and a crisp edging, the informal lawn lends itself to a more naturalistic treatment. Here a limited number of shrub varieties can serve as a background and enclosure. A few small flowering trees will improve the border's outline, while a foreground and underplanting of ground cover with a gentle flowing edge separates lawn and boundary. Shrub borders also serve as a framework, providing sides and a lowered foreground for a view; the tree shading the terrace may also help. On smaller properties, where space does not permit a naturalistic border, an architectural pattern of plant arrangement is more appropriate.

The third dimension—height—is limited by the firmament overhead, which may be somewhat out of proportion to the size of a small plot. Most people feel more comfortable with the suggestion of something overhead. Trees were man's first shelters, and they still contribute greatly to our comfort by deflecting, absorbing and reducing the sun's radiation and glare, and by reducing noise. As elements of design, trees are the most valuable of plant forms; one tree, well chosen and properly located, will accomplish more than a forest of shrubs. Trees complement the house, frame it, cast shadows upon it, soften its hard lines and balance it with landscape elements of similar importance. Architecturally they may serve as walls, colonnades, roofs, or canopies. Trees of limited height may be used in quantity in rows or patterns 10 feet apart,

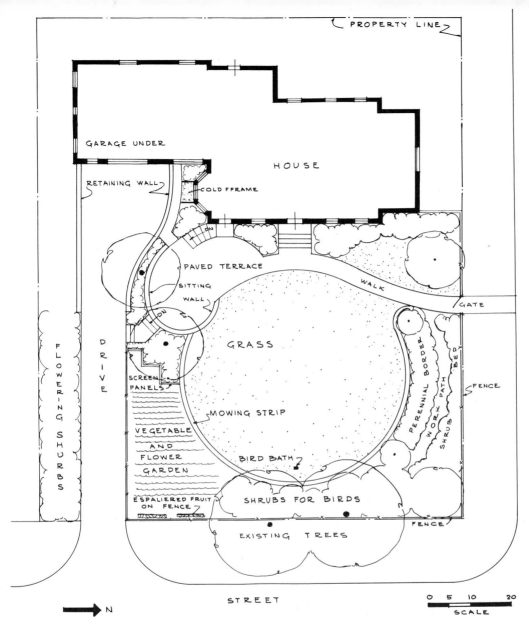

PROPERTY LINE

GARAGE UNDER

HOUSE

RETAINING WALL

COLD FFRAME

PAVED TERRACE

SITTING WALL

WALK

GATE

F L O W E R I N G   S H U R B S

D R I V E

GRASS

SCREEN PANELS

MOWING STRIP

VEGETABLE AND FLOWER GARDEN

BIRD BATH

PERENNIAL BORDER

WORK PATH

SHRUB BED

FENCE

ESPALIERED FRUIT ON FENCE

SHRUBS FOR BIRDS

FENCE

EXISTING   TREES

STREET

N

0 5 10 20
SCALE

157. *In this city landscape the only
usable outdoor space, measuring 70 by
80 feet, is located between the house
and the street; the house is set well to
the rear of the rectangular lot with
deliveries accessible from the side
street. An existing driveway along the
south property line leads to a two-car
garage beneath the house. The entire
front space, except for the drive, was
enclosed with a fence to provide
privacy. The main entrance to the
house was used as the axis and center
line for a circular grass panel
providing the major open space in the
garden. This is edged with a mowing
strip for easy maintenance but it also
helps to accentuate the crisp circular
form. Access to the entrance is
provided by a gentle curved walk from
the side street. A free-form terrace
shaded by two existing trees has its
own entrance to the house. Since the
land slopes toward the drive, a low
sitting wall helps to offset the change
of grade. The terrace looks out on the
lawn panel, the birdbath and bird
sanctuary of berried shrubs grouped
beneath existing trees and the main
garden to the south. A vegetable and
cutting garden with espaliered fruits
trained against the enclosing fence
is set between driveway and lawn.*

169

or treated as a small woodland, combining the function of enclosure and canopy.

Trees grow tall enough to provide the good proportions so needed in the three-dimensional landscape. Deciduous varieties are best in the garden and as complements of domestic architecture. But beware of overdoing a good thing. A shade tree 30 to 50 feet high will eventually dominate a 50-foot property. Since shade trees should not cover more than half the available space, one or two full-sized trees are often sufficient for a small place. Just as the sky is more interesting when there is a contrast of sky and clouds, so is the lawn more attractive when the expanse of sun-drenched grass is decorated with shadow patterns cast by trees. Shadows help to delineate the form of the land and the objects upon it. Continuous changes in light alter shadow pattern, form, color,

158. *Enclosure and canopy are the outdoor equivalent of walls and ceiling, giving us boundary, privacy and a sense of shelter.*

texture and mood. In winter, welcome sunlight streams through the bare crown. Sidelighting outlines the structure of trunk, branch and twig; the shadow pattern of the whole tree is a design in itself.

Few situations are more discouraging than a landscape without sunlight. Old houses are often surrounded by beautiful old trees casting such heavy shade in summer that the interior is sunless. Even worse is a house with a galaxy of big spruce or pine; rarely does sunlight cross the threshold. Trees that do this should be removed.

The sheltering function of the house roof may be extended into the garden by means of structures. The choice is extensive: porch, arbor, pergola, trellis, overhead slatting, etcetera. These provide varying degrees of shade or alternating patterns of moving sunlight and shade, and may be decorated with vines.

159. *In suburban areas, a screening fence secures privacy and also serves as windbreak. In summer the trees provide the cooling canopy overhead.*

160. *The size and substance of the enclosure should be appropriate to the need and in proper scale. As a property needs enclosure, so may a particular area like a flower garden.*

161. *If space is minimal, as in a city garden, fencing is the best investment for privacy.*

162. *A tall maple complements the architecture of this house in what seems to be a plenitude of canopy.*

164 (below left). *A hedge is used to limit a view, giving a feeling of containment and protection, and focusing attention on a vista.*

163 (below right). *A tree provides the overhead tracery that completes the frame.*

11

PULLING IT ALL TOGETHER

Landscape design as an art form cannot be taught by means of dogmatic rules. Fortunately, there is always more than one possible solution in developing any site, and a plan on paper should be regarded merely as a device for studying a variety of approaches. When a solution works nicely on paper, it can be staked out on the ground and then adjusted or rejected accordingly. To be of any help, a plan must be drawn to scale or correct proportion. A scale of $\frac{1}{8}$ inch $= 1$ foot is convenient for solving the average landscape problem.

The reasonably level land shown in Drawing 165 is approximately three-quarters of an acre with a frontage of 150 feet on the south side of a northwest-southeast street. The setback line is 50 feet from house to street. The two-story house has a living room, dining room, family room and kitchen on the first floor, and an attached two-car garage. The orientation is unusual in that the sun enters all windows of the house at some hour of the day; only the north corners of house and garage are not touched by the sun's rays. (One school of thought considers such a diagonal arrangement superior to solar orientation in which the main living space faces south.)

The public space includes the land lying between the front of the house and street, enough area to provide a pleasant setting for the house and a safe, workable off-the-street parking area. The scheme shown will accommodate four guest cars without obstructing the drive. The drive itself is uncluttered, with clear visibility in both directions. Since no backing out is required, it has a pleasant flowing line, far more attractive than the usual straight driveway. Cars park head-in toward the side property line, and do not detract from the view of the house. There is room for screen planting to separate parked cars from the next property. The short walk from drive to front door has a comfortable width of 4½ feet and all-weather surface; it leads to an adequate landing, 5 by 7 feet, with a minimum of correctly designed steps. The service entrance is connected with the drive at the front of the garage. *175*

The front lawn, separated from planting beds by a mowing strip, is simple and uncluttered; it is set at the same level as the drive to minimize edging and trimming. Trees along the drive help subordinate the garage and parking court. Planting against the house is simple: the front entrance is accented with a pair of specimen evergreens and the corners softened with appropriate plants. These are tied together with beds of ground cover and low-growing evergreens. A tree near the southeast corner casts a pleasant morning shadow pattern across the lawn; flowering trees and shrubs behind a flowing mow line divide the front space from the garden southeast of the house.

The logical location for the service area is between the garage and the property line. Paved with the same surface as the drive and parking court, it is screened on three sides with a fence or wall of the same material and construction as the garage. It provides weatherproof storage for garage cans and all those miscellaneous items that so often clutter up the garage to the extent that cars can hardly squeeze in. Since vehicular access to the private part of the property can be convenient or necessary, a double-leaf gate is provided on two sides of the service yard. For daily use a single-leaf gate is in operation; it is wide enough for a wheelbarrow to be pushed through without scraping two sets of knuckles.

The southwest part of the house, with living and family rooms, opens onto a paved rectangular terrace, 18 by 30 feet, in accordance with the golden mean formula. A planting bed between the house and the terrace gives year-round interest and helps to break up the hard paved look. The adjoining smaller dining terrace, 12 by 18 feet, is handy to the kitchen. A special feature is the shady arbor at the end of this terrace with a small wall fountain and pool attached to the garage. This combined living-dining terrace is shaded by two carefully placed deciduous trees providing afternoon shade in summer but allowing winter sun to warm the house.

Terrace and living room look southeastward into the garden. Since

PULLING IT ALL TOGETHER

garden and terrace are intimately related to the house, they are purposely geometric in form. In contrast to the two golden mean rectangles of the terrace, the garden combines a circle and an octagon. It is basically simple, with a strong year-round form. A crisp edging outlines the neat grass panel and provides the foreground for beds of bulbs and flowers. A green garden with low shrubs or ground cover, or a combination of both, are other pleasing solutions. A neat circle of small flowering trees or handsome evergreens gives enclosure and background, while providing privacy from the neighbors.

The largest portion of this outdoor living space is treated informally with the suggestion of an elliptical lawn area leading the eye to the view beyond. Three shade trees add height and suggest shelter; they also cast attractive shadow patterns across the sunny oval lawn. The enclosing band of planting on the southeast and southwest property lines is made up of small flowering trees, evergreens and flowering shrubs, tied together with an underplanting of ground cover material and shade-loving wildflowers of the forest floor. Such a boundary planting, offering cover and food for birds, will in turn help with the insect problem. A rustic bench may be placed in a quiet spot for bird watching. There can also be an informal pool with a shallow portion for the birds and a deeper part for aquatic plants.

The view from the terrace is framed by tall trees; the planting between them should be kept as low as possible, to form a green base for the view. Since it is open to the southwest, it should funnel summer breezes into the outdoor living room.

Pleasant as it is, a private space of this size can accommodate another feature, a garden house located at the end of the view from the kitchen window. Here it will serve as a focal point, terminating a garden path of brick. It also serves as an interlude in a walk around the property by foot, since it joins a stepping stone path meandering along the informal shrub border and leading to the southeast garden off the main terrace.

A paved terrace with a barbecue and hi-fi will provide diversion, and so will space on the lawn for a badminton court. If the family is garden-oriented, the terminal feature can be a tool house with a clematis bower and a work terrace. A cultivated bed west of the path from terrace to tool house would furnish cut flowers from spring through fall. Three or four blueberry bushes, dwarf fruit trees or specimen hollies, repeated at intervals, will make it attractive in winter.

If the family wishes to grow its own vegetables, there is a perfect spot along the northwest property line. Here is adequate space for everything—flowers for cutting, herbs, vegetables of all kinds, even sweet corn, with room left over for asparagus, strawberries and raspberries, plus space for a compost pit and a cold frame at the rear. This working garden can be separated from the main lawn by grape vines trained on wires; one or two fruit trees may shade the tool house and terrace.

For families that cannot live without a swimming pool the garden plot is a perfect spot for it. For safety's sake it is fenced on all sides. The garden-tool house now becomes a pool and bath house, and the terrace a sunbathing spot.

An alternate scheme would develop this northwest segment as multiple-use space. A family with small children can use the portion southwest of the garage as a play area. The usual clutter of wading pool, sandbox, swing and slide equipment, enclosed by a see-through fence, is within ear-shot of mother yet not too obtrusive. Those who have dogs may use this space for a run, with a dog door leading to a sheltered space inside the garage. There is no reason why this space could not combine an above-ground swimming pool, play equipment, and some garden beds while leaving the pristine effect of lawn, informal enclosure, garden and terrace untrammeled. A similar combination can be used on most home grounds, regardless of size—the principles need merely be adapted to suit the family, the house and the property.

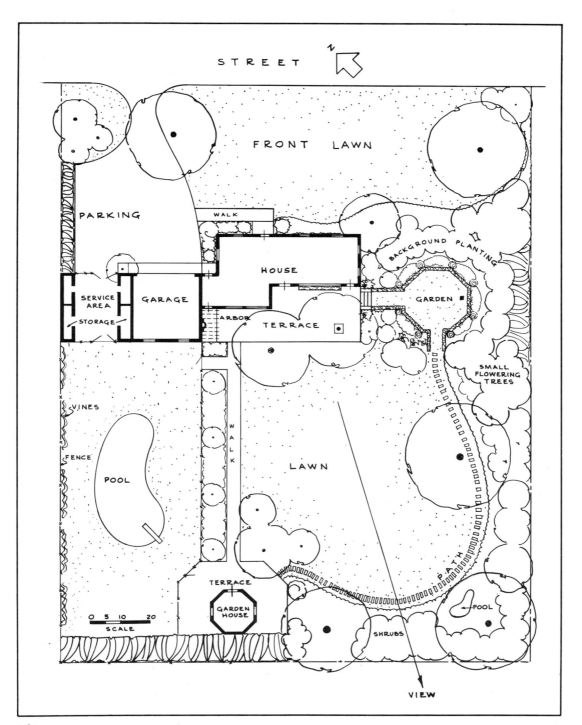

STREET

FRONT LAWN

PARKING

WALK

SERVICE AREA

STORAGE

GARAGE

HOUSE

BACKGROUND PLANTING

GARDEN

ARBOR

TERRACE

SMALL FLOWERING TREES

VINES

FENCE

POOL

WALK

LAWN

PATH

TERRACE

GARDEN HOUSE

O 5 10 20
SCALE

SHRUBS

POOL

VIEW

165.

III
LANDSCAPE DESIGN TAKES PRACTICAL SHAPE

12

HOW TO IMPROVE YOUR CURVES

Form is a vital part of the landscape. The designer, as well as the home gardener blessed with an artistic eye, is aware of the shape of a terrace or lawn, the pattern of a garden or flower bed, the form of a specimen tree, a shrub or a towering delphinium.

Form and line are inseparable, for line—straight and/or curved—defines or outlines the form. The landscape architect is interested in a beautiful line wherever it occurs: in a parkway or driveway, a path, the edging of a flower bed, a fence line or a shrub border as it joins the lawn.

Engineers speak of lines as alignment. As far as I know, no one has set down any suggestions on the aesthetics of alignment. The ones indicated below are my own, based on years of work in public and private landscape design. The same principles that make a parkway pleasant to look at, easy and safe to travel on, can improve the home drive and the garden walk. A garden path with pleasing alignment costs no more than one of clumsy design, and a very small refinement can often make the difference.

The simplest kind of curve is the *circular curve,* part of a circle a schoolboy makes with his first compass. It has a center and a radius, as shown in Drawing 167.

When a straight line, called a tangent, is added to a curve, it forms a 90 degree angle with the radius of the curve. (See Drawing 168.)

The second kind of curve is the *compound curve.* It travels in one direction but is made up of two or more circular curves, each with a different radius and center. If a wedge of an 8-inch pie is placed beside a wedge of a 9-inch pie with the outer edges neatly joined, they will form a compound curve. (See Drawing 169.)

Compound curves have many uses in the landscape. If carefully designed, they are graceful and flowing. To insure this effect, we join circular curves directly, for a compound curve loses its fluid character when the curves are joined by means of a tangent or straight line, resulting in an unattractive "broken back" effect, as in Drawing 170.

166. *A curve gives form, and form is far more satisfying than disarray. This brick walk repeats the curve of the terrace shown in drawing 210.*

HOW TO IMPROVE YOUR CURVES

In the landscape the compound curve makes an excellent transition or connector. For instance, when a driveway joins a public road more or less at a right angle, a much more pleasant alignment results if the straight driveway is gradually eased into the opposing straight line of the public road with a compound curve composed of curving segments with progressively shorter radii. (See Drawing 171.)

If the radii of a compound curve become regularly and progressively longer or shorter, the curve approaches a spiral. Rams' horns and seashells are natural spirals. (See Drawing 172.)

Another common type of curve is the *reverse curve* that travels first in one direction, then in the opposite. This is the most difficult to do well. All too often in the home landscape it becomes just a wiggly line. However, no other well designed curve can add as much interest, grace and motion; it is a line going someplace, beautifully. The reverse curve is the most important in today's highways, but it is also used to edge a shrub border, a flower bed, a terrace or a lawn. It can be the center line of a fence, a drive, a walk or a stepping-stone path.

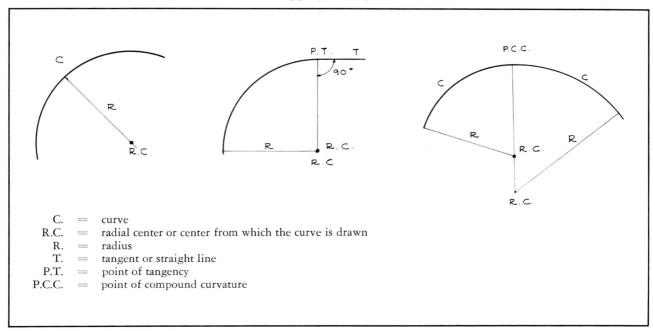

C.	=	curve
R.C.	=	radial center or center from which the curve is drawn
R.	=	radius
T.	=	tangent or straight line
P.T.	=	point of tangency
P.C.C.	=	point of compound curvature

167, 168 and 169. *Circular curve; curve with tangent; compound curve.*

For a reverse curve, a short tangent is always needed to connect the two opposing curves. This gives the eye a second to adjust itself before sweeping off in the opposite direction (Drawing 174), a subtle refinement of line often overlooked by layman and engineers alike. It can make the difference between a smooth flowing line and a wiggly one. Compare the curves in Drawing 175, joined together abruptly, and the same curves in Drawing 174, connected by a short transitional tangent which makes a much more pleasant reverse curve.

A second way to design attractive reverse curves is to use long gentle curves and short tangents, as illustrated in Drawing 176. Long tangents and a short curve result in a choppy, sometimes wiggly line, as in Drawing 177. In both cases, points A and B are in the same location and the tangent direction is the same, but most will agree that the more pleasant route from A to B is shown in Drawing 176.

So far, we have been concerned with horizontal curves, those laid flat on the ground and moving right or left. But roads go uphill, over the crest and downhill by means of vertical curves. Curves with changes of elevation are equally important in the landscape. A good reverse curve turned on its side becomes an *ogee curve,* and is the most attractive profile to use in grading a sloping piece of land or a steep bank. (See Chapter 13.)

In such a case there is a broad gentle curve at the top of the slope, a short straight tangent in the middle of it and a broad gentle curve flowing in the opposite direction at the foot, as in Drawing 179. There is no awkward straight line effect as there would be if flat terraces at the top and bottom were joined by a straight slope, as shown in Drawing 180.

The ogee curve should be used on a walk or driveway which goes up- or downgrade. As the car climbs the slope, the gentle curve and easy leveling off is safe and convenient for getting in and out of the garage. Travelling down the slope, this gradual leveling off is an important safety factor as the car enters the street.

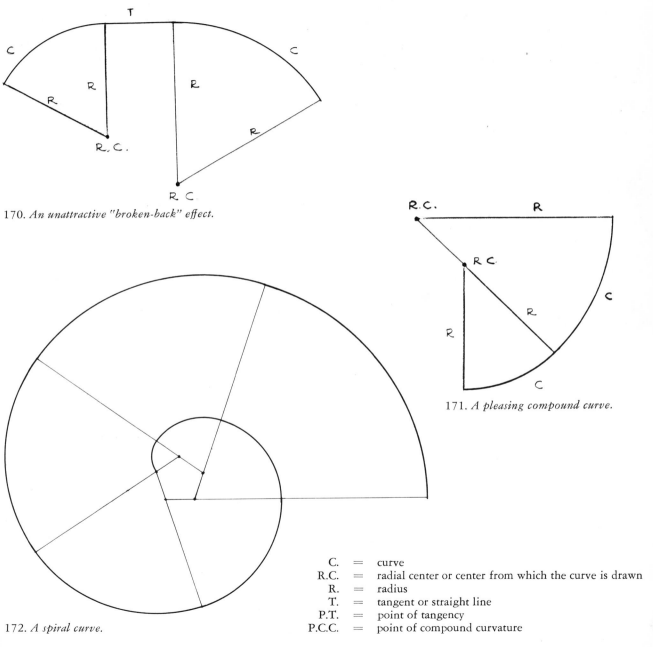

170. *An unattractive "broken-back" effect.*

171. *A pleasing compound curve.*

172. *A spiral curve.*

C.	=	curve
R.C.	=	radial center or center from which the curve is drawn
R.	=	radius
T.	=	tangent or straight line
P.T.	=	point of tangency
P.C.C.	=	point of compound curvature

187

173. *A reverse curve has many uses in landscaping, as in this border.*

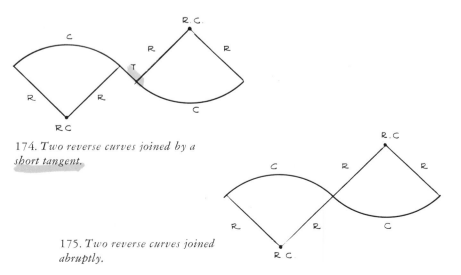

174. *Two reverse curves joined by a short tangent.*

175. *Two reverse curves joined abruptly.*

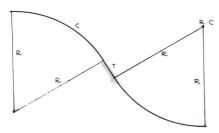

176. *Long gentle curves and short tangents*

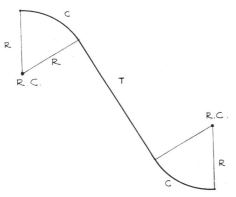

177. *Long tangents and short curves.*

178. *Another adaptation of the reverse curve. This walk with graceful iris beds on either side takes a sharp turn to the right and adjoins a terrace.*

179. *An ogee curve makes an attractive profile for a slope.*

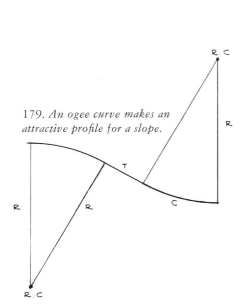

180. *Awkward straight line slope.*

13

GRADING OR SHAPING THE LAND'S SURFACE

Many a house is built with scarcely a thought to the finished grade of the land surrounding it. Some are set high with 3 or 4 feet of concrete foundation exposed. Others are too low and become surrounded by a pond in heavy rain. A steep bank behind the house may keep the cellar continually damp, because no thought has been given to proper drainage. In the usual building routine the bulldozer digs the cellar hole; the contractor builds the house and throws construction debris against the foundation; the bulldozer returns and spreads the cellar dirt into a terrace around the house. Or, he may level off the whole lot, destroying all natural slopes and existing plants. It is now ready for something known as "landscaping." Alas, it may already be too late for salvation.

Landscape design is concerned with the three dimensions of outdoor space. Few pieces of land are completely flat; there is usually a slight change of grade which represents the height. Elsewhere there may be abrupt changes of elevation, with slopes up, down or crosswise. Some grading is required in developing most properties since reasonably level areas are needed on which to build, park, sit, play or garden. Walks, roads and drives also need to be fairly level, so grading is often required to make them workable. Grading for drainage is most important, for water must be carried away from buildings and off walks, terraces, roads and parking areas. In fact, while it may seem like an expensive operation, nothing is more vital to the appearance and maintenance of a site than well-thought-out grading.

Minor refinements do not always require heavy machinery. Like a child in a sandbox, one may sometimes model the surface by hand, using a shovel and wheelbarrow. Today grading is usually done by earthmoving machinery and special operators, but it is wise for the homeowner to understand the principles which underlie shaping the earth's surface for usability, safety, drainage and beauty. Though some engineering is involved, a sizeable amount of grading is based on practical common sense.

The proposed development of house site should include a grading *191* plan or study based on a topographic survey of the property—a scale drawing showing the property lines, the street or road with its legally established elevations, the contours indicating the slope of the land, and the physical features: buildings, trees, rock outcrops, streams, swamps, etcetera. The grading plan will take into consideration the terrain and the changes that will be needed in building the house and installing the landscape features. It will show the relationship between street level, house and garage floor levels and the respective levels of terraces, lawns, gardens, together with their relation to the existing unalterable grades along each property line. Proposed changes in the surface will be indicated—the necessary cuts and fills, walls and slopes and the required drainage. An attempt is usually made to balance the cuts (soil removed) and fills (soil added) so that no soil need be carted away nor extra amounts brought in. (See Drawing 198.)

Land should not be bullied; it should be respected for what it is— a bit of ancient geology battered for ages by physical forces and only now threatened by man and the bulldozer. Grading does not mean reducing the earth's surface to a flat plane. All grading operations should conform somewhat to the terrain; a site may be altered to serve a specific need and may sometimes be improved, but it is unwise to completely remake it. The different levels which naturally exist can add interest and charm, though they may present certain limitations when locating the house, the drive and parking areas. Rough spots may be smoothed, but the finished product should resemble attractive natural forms. It is no accident that many parks, parkways, public areas and private places have pleasant slopes and gentle undulations, merging and blending man-made landscapes with existing surfaces; many of these have been constructed from grading plans.

When building a new house on an unimproved site, each operation will follow in logical order if some advance thought has been given to the finished form of land surfaces and the elevations of house floor and related outdoor features. First, the existing trees must be adequately protected, not only against physical damage to the trunks but also against soil compacting over their roots. This means a strong barricade to protect the entire area under the spread of the branches and to exclude all traffic. Any cut or fill around trees should be done beyond the drip line; either a slope or a wall may be used to support the change in grade.

Then the existing topsoil should be stripped and stockpiled where it will not be disturbed. All areas involved in construction of the house, terrace, drive and parking areas as well as adjacent land disturbed by machinery, storage of materials and construction activities should be stripped to subsoil level. This is an important step. Too often the soil from the cellar excavation is leveled off around the house and the owner is left with the problem of making a lawn on subsoil and construction debris.

Wherever possible, utility lines should be buried. When construction is complete, the subsoil surface should be molded and shaped according to its final landscape role. If badly compacted, it may be loosened by roto-tilling before returning the topsoil. The topsoil itself should be spread in varying depths for different areas: 6 inches for lawn areas; 12 inches for ground cover; 18 inches for flower beds; 24 inches for shrub borders and 36 inches for trees. It is wise to add one-fifth extra to compensate for settling, unless soil is compacted as it is spread.

Grading operations are of utmost importance and the owner should check as they progress to avoid future headaches. Safe and easy access and proper drainage are absolutely vital, and both depend upon correct shaping of land surface.

Grading must first solve drainage problems so that water does not stand anywhere. Whenever possible, existing drainage patterns should be respected and used to advantage. These patterns are most apparent in early spring when the frost is coming out of the ground—one can see then where water comes from and where it goes.

Drainage works best if water is kept on the move, but not too rapidly lest it cause erosion. Grass or ground cover helps prevent excess washing. A grass surface should be pitched 2 per cent, or a vertical drop of 2 feet in a run of 100 feet in horizontal distance. (See Drawing 185.) This will appear to be level, but it will move water slowly, allowing a sizeable amount to sink into the soil. In porous soil the pitch may be reduced to 1 per cent. Near buildings or in areas where water should never accumulate, it may be wise to increase the pitch to 3 per cent (3 feet of vertical drop in a horizontal run of 100 feet), since it will move water efficiently and still appear nearly level to the eye. If the surrounding land slopes steeply, the lawn grade may be increased to 6 per cent. Wherever possible, slopes to be maintained in lawn should be no steeper than 20 per cent (20 feet of drop in a run of 100 feet, or a drop of 1 foot in 5 feet of horizontal distance). In meadows the slope may be increased to 30 per cent.

Unfortunately, it is not always possible to disperse all surface water in this manner. Water rushing down a steep slope will cut gullies; here a ditch at the top of the bank and at right angles to it will intercept water from higher up and will move it safely away at a slower speed. In many situations a swale or shallow grass gutter should be formed at the base of a bank. This picks up water falling on the slopes and carries it away gradually.

All areas should be pitched or tilted so that water moves slowly off their surfaces. The easiest way is to tilt the surface in one direction so that water flows off the low side. If this will result in an undesirable concentration of water, a swale or valley with a 2 per cent pitch should carry it away to a catch basin or other disposal point. Large paved areas sometimes have the low point in the center where water is drained off and piped away.

It is most important to make sure that water drains away from all buildings. The most critical situation arises when the land slopes down to a building. Here the solution is to cut into the slope, tilting the cut slope away from the building so that water flows away from the foundation. This collected water must be carried away by means of a valley or swale with at least a 2 per cent pitch.

Hopefully the day is past when a new house is surrounded by a steep narrow terrace of clay from the cellar excavavation. (See Drawing 188.) The ideal grading scheme for the average house and lot would place the floor level of the house above the grade of the street. There should always be at least one step down from the threshold of the door to the outside landing, terrace or walk.

Wooden houses should have at least 6 inches of exposed foundation *below* the base of the wood. This means that the first floor elevation must be kept at least 18 inches above the earth around the foundation. In houses built on a concrete floor slab the earth should be kept at least 7 inches below the first floor level. The walk and lawn surface should then slope gently down and away from the house, with enough pitch to move surface water away from the foundation. As it moves away from the building, the gentle slope rolls down in a long gentle ogee curve (described on page 186), which provides a maximum amount of visible lawn area. This curve may be quite steep and still look well, if there is enough space between the house and street. Even a slight curve is more attractive there than a straight line, and a long gentle curve is always more pleasant than a combination of a straight line and a steep bank. The steepness of a front slope can also be reduced by using a terrace along the house front, supported by a retaining wall plus an ogee curve as before. The height of this wall may be subordinated by planting against it.

A different problem exists when the floor level of the house is below street level. If the grade pitches water against the house foundation, nothing but grief can follow. An ogee curve is used to drop the grade from the curb to a low point well away from the house if space permits, closer if space is limited, but always lower than the grade at the foundation. This moves water away from the house and out to the low point. The low point must also pitch crosswise so that water is gently carried toward—or around—one or both sides of the property.

If none of these solutions is possible, water should be picked up with a catch basin located at the low spot, and carried away by a drain. The house with floor level below the street can also use a terrace supported by a retaining wall to meet the higher grade of the front lawn; this visually cuts off a portion of the base of the house as seen from the street, which may or may not be a disadvantage.

A lawn area may be graded in a number of ways (see Chapter 7). It may be treated as a plane and tilted or pitched at least 2 per cent to permit water flow; this is an easy but unimaginative solution. As we have seen, the most interesting lawn form is saucer shape, since the entire area can be seen. Runoff can be achieved by tilting the saucer slightly so water drains out the front or the side. A large flat expanse of space can be made more interesting by a minor change of grade. A large house overlooking a flat lawn was given a curved grass terrace sweeping out from each side of the house and swelling into a full-blown feature bounded by a brick wall 8 inches high, with a mowing strip along the base. Seen from the lawn, the house appeared to be resting on a low curving platform of generous proportions, neatly edged by a minimal brick wall which added an architectural note and cast a small shadow, all achieved through a slight change of grade in an otherwise flat expanse.

In other locations usable level land may be at a premium or sites may be difficult to develop due to uphill, downhill or crosshill slopes. A property serves best if there is reasonably level space near the house to provide access by foot and by car and be used for various outdoor activities. This may involve more than simple reshaping of existing topography.

A slope can be made reasonably level by three methods: (1) cutting into the bank, (2) filling out from the bank, or (3) a combination of the two. Cutting into a bank provides a stable surface on which to build, and cut slopes can also be steeper than filled ones. Low spots may sometimes be levelled or a small level area be enlarged by the addition of fill or soil brought in. However, filled slopes erode since the soil is loose, and they can never be as steep as cut ones. A house built on a filled slope must have its foundation extended through the fill into undisturbed subsoil—an expensive operation. Whenever possible, a new level should be a combination of cut and fill. Soil excavated for the house may be used to bring lower areas up to usable levels, and no soil need be brought in nor hauled away.

Sites which slope down from street level create an illusion of a much larger space, though they may present problems in screening out undesirable views. Here is an opportunity to develop garden and grass spaces to be enjoyed from the house, porch or terrace. Gardens on successive levels can often be more attractive and unusual than those confined to a single level.

If the change of grade is considerable, a recreation room at the basement level can open directly out onto a terrace, while the living room can open onto a wooden deck one story above, with steps leading down to ground level. The slope here can usually be made far less steep and an acceptable level on the downhill or private side of the house can be achieved by using soil removed from the house excavation. Or the house may be set high in front, and soil taken from the front lawn can be used for a terrace in back. A most attractive treatment consists of two or three levels stepping down in turn; these are separated by low retaining walls and generous, easy steps so that traveling from one level to another is a pleasant adventure. These levels might feature sitting areas, lawn panels or garden beds with flowering trees or shrubs, as needed. These flower beds should be designed to be attractive when viewed from above. Water features can be used economically and effectively on a downhill site since water can be reused, as it flows by gravity.

Often portions of sloping sites can be left unaltered. A small orchard of dwarf fruit trees or a garden of berry bushes lend themselves to sloping terrain. Rows should follow the contour so that erosion is kept at a minimum. Even a well-mulched vegetable garden can be maintained on a slope if the rows follow the contours, running across the slope rather than up and down hill. Even more interest can be achieved in a small vegetable or cutting garden by using railroad ties as a stepped divider.

Land sloping away from the house less steeply may be reshaped to permit two or more relatively level spaces devoted to different uses. The upper level adjoining the house may include a paved sitting area with a low sitting wall along the outer edge which doubles as retaining wall, supporting the grade as it drops in elevation. Steps may lead to an intermediate level in grass or garden, or to a swimming pool terrace. Beyond that a bank sloping down to the existing grade at the back line can be covered with enclosing screen planting.

An uphill property can be difficult to develop if the slope is steep. Here one must try for an outlook that gives a feeling of spaciousness. Usually a level sitting area and at least some lawn can be achieved with a fair balance of cut and fill if the house floor level is wisely chosen. Soil excavated for a combined garden and terrace can be used as fill for the front of the house, which stands somewhat above street level (usually the garage would be located under the house). This outdoor living space should be at least 25 feet wide and should extend the entire width of the house. The cut-out portion on the uphill side should have a wall of minimum height to support the slope above. The upper garden should be in grass beginning at the top of the wall, so the eye drinks in the sun-and shadow-patterned open space. Such a lawn can be framed at sides and back by informal curved planting beds of flowering trees and shrubs, with higher planting at the back if screening is needed. Steps extending into the upper level invite exploration of an upper garden. In many cases, such an upper level may be the undisturbed existing terrain.

A third situation is the property that slopes crosswise from one side to the other. This lends itself to an ideal plot plan and has excellent

possibilities, especially if there is a view. The change in elevation across the front of the lot is usually no more than 4 to 8 feet at most. Perhaps two thirds of the width can be graded to a fairly level lawn and garden related to the living room on the upper side. The lower portion may be used for service, utility garden, driveway or parking. A wall or planted bank may separate the two areas.

Abrupt changes of grade may be handled in two ways: by using a retaining wall or by a sloping bank of earth. The most attractive and easily maintained separation is achieved by a wall, though it may cost more. Walls add interest by providing an architectural feature in the garden and may serve as focal points, while casting shadow patterns of a crisper nature than are achieved by foliage alone. Furthermore, walls are usually associated with steps which reinforce and enhance the design suggesting movement and progression.

Cut or filled slopes are cheaper to install, but present a maintenance problem. The angle of repose asumed by an unsupported pile of dirt depends upon the type of soil. Heavy soils may be cut as steeply as 1 to 1, or 1 foot of drop in 1 foot of horizontal distance—a 100 per cent slope. In areas of fill the maximum is 2 to 1, or 1 foot of drop in 2 feet of horizontal distance. All filled slopes must be compacted and water diverted from the top or they will promptly erode. Steep slopes should be covered with paving or planting as soon as possible. Such maximum slopes are unattractive and require considerable care to prevent washing, hence should be used only when space is at a premium. Some steep slopes can be improved by using stepped railroad ties and planting, but this is an expensive solution. If a slope is inevitable, use more space and make it long and gentle, rounded at top and bottom, forming an ogee curve. A 7 to 1 slope is pleasant to look at and can be easily maintained in grass. The maximum slope for grass should be 4 to 1. Three to 1 slopes are hard to maintain and should be planted with tough ground cover. This can be costly, with two years of weeding and watering of young plants before they can be considered self-maintaining.

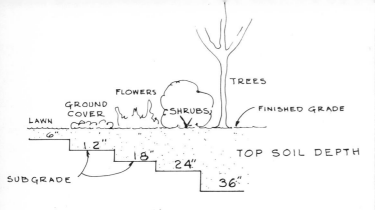

TREES

FLOWERS

GROUND
COVER

SHRUBS

FINISHED GRADE

LAWN

6"

12"

18"

24"

36"

TOP SOIL DEPTH

SUBGRADE

SECTION

181. *Optimum topsoil depths for
different kinds of plant material.*

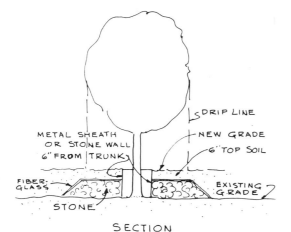

DRIP LINE

METAL SHEATH
OR STONE WALL
6" FROM TRUNK

NEW GRADE

6" TOP SOIL

FIBER-
GLASS

STONE

EXISTING
GRADE

SECTION

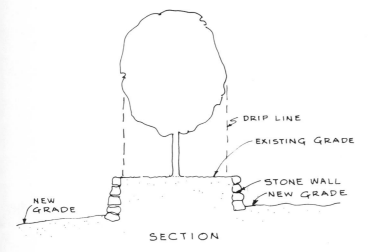

DRIP LINE

EXISTING GRADE

STONE WALL
NEW GRADE

NEW
GRADE

SECTION

182 (left center). *If fill must be added to raise the grade under
a tree, a metal sheath or circular wall of stone should be placed
around the trunk and at least 6 inches away from it. Stone or
gravel should be spread over the existing surface to within
6 inches of the new grade, and covered with a fiberglass blanket
to keep out the soil but allow water and air to pass through.
Topsoil may then be spread over the fiberglass.*

183 (left). *No grading should be done under the spread of a
tree. If the grade must be lowered by cutting, support the
existing grade under the tree with a circular dry stone wall.*

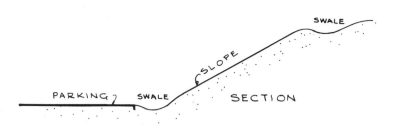

186. *Slopes should be designed so they do not dump water onto used areas. Here a swale or shallow grass gutter intercepts the runoff from the slope and carries it around the parking area. A valley or swale at the top of the slope will carry away water slowly and prevent it from running down and eroding the bank.*

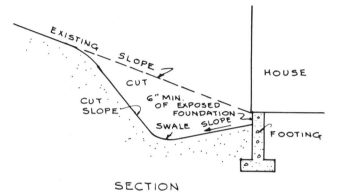

187. *Water should never be allowed to drain toward a building. A cut should be made so that the land slopes away from the building's foundation. A swale will carry water around the building, or a catch basin may be installed.*

184 (above). *Proper grading is basic and should be carefully checked. Water in a cellar or puddling where it is not wanted can be a real headache and costly to correct. A change in grade between house and driveway can be accomplished by a stone wall, giving the house a pleasing setting while taking care of the grading. Many people use railroad ties for this purpose.*

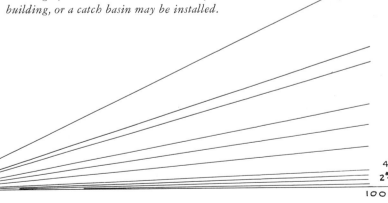

185 (right). *Slopes for the landscape.*
1 per cent slope—minimum for drainage of paved areas
2 per cent slope
3 per cent slope } *For lawn areas*
4 per cent slope
20 per cent slope—maximum slope for lawn area
30 per cent slope—maximum slope for maintained landscape

201

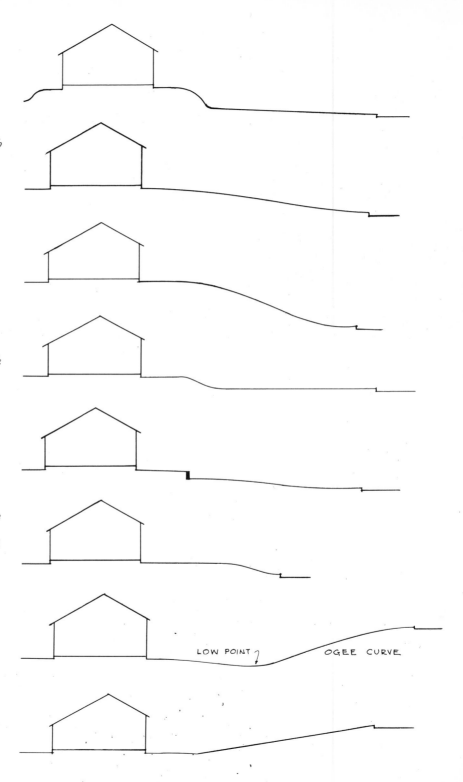

188. *This house sits unpleasantly insecure, perched on a mound of subsoil excavated from the basement.*

189. *The ideal profile is one in which the house is slightly above the street level; the lawn is graded toward the street in a long gentle ogee curve.*

190. *This slope profile may be quite steep and still look attractive if space is adequate.*

191. *The long gentle slope shown in Drawing 189 is more attractive and easier to maintain than the steep bank and flat lawn shown here.*

192. *Here a terrace reduces the steepness of the slope.*

193. *On lots where the house must be placed high because of sewer line connections, it is better to have a wall or sloping bank at the property line.*

194. *When the street is higher than the house level an ogee curve may be used, with the low point kept well away from the house.*

LOW POINT OGEE CURVE

195. *An example of an unattractive slope with the low point too close to the house.*

196. *In this interesting change of grade, the garden is three easy steps below the grass terrace.*

197. *A house on an expanse of level land was given a new setting by adding a sizeable semicircular grass terrace supported by a brick wall 8 inches high. (See photograph 200.)*

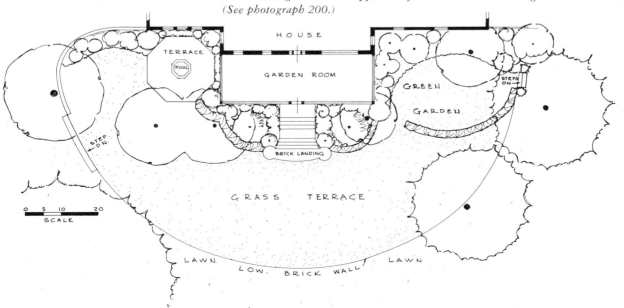

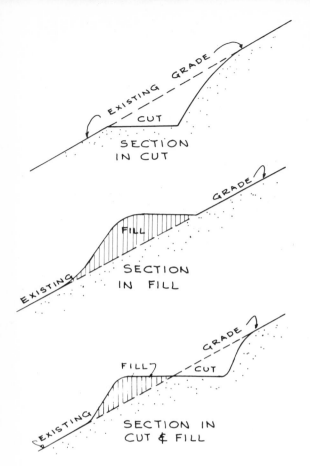

198. *Three ways in which a level area may be achieved on a slope.*

199. *The steep slope on the right was cut and supported by a retaining wall along the driveway. Dense ground cover prevents erosion.*

200 (below). *A side view of the elevated brick-curbed grass terrace shown in drawing 197.*

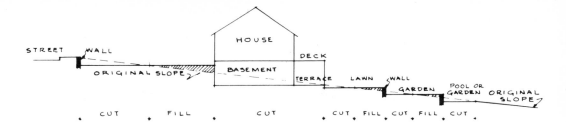

STREET · WALL · ORIGINAL SLOPE · HOUSE · BASEMENT · DECK · TERRACE · LAWN · WALL · GARDEN · POOL OR GARDEN · ORIGINAL SLOPE

CUT · FILL · CUT · CUT · FILL · CUT · FILL · CUT

201. *The house on a steep downhill slope might have a terrace outside a basement recreation room, or a wooden deck off the main floor level. Low walls are used to separate reasonably level areas for lawn or garden which result in a good balance of cut and fill.*

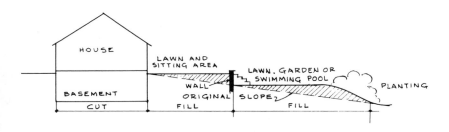

HOUSE · BASEMENT · LAWN AND SITTING AREA · LAWN, GARDEN OR SWIMMING POOL · PLANTING · WALL · ORIGINAL SLOPE · CUT · FILL · FILL

202. *Soil removed from cellar excavation was used to develop two level areas—a sitting area supported by a retaining wall which doubles as a sitting wall at the terrace level, and below, a lawn or swimming pool terrace with a planted slope used in place of a wall.*

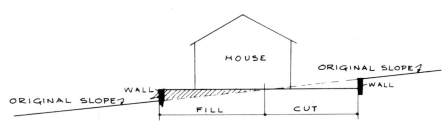

PUBLIC AREA · STREET · HOUSE · LAWN & TERRACE · WALL · LAWN OR GARDEN ON ORIGINAL SLOPE · FILL · CUT

203. *The house on an uphill slope has a generous outdoor living area adjacent to the house supported by a retaining wall. The upper slope should have grass to the top of the wall, giving a pleasant feeling of openness.*

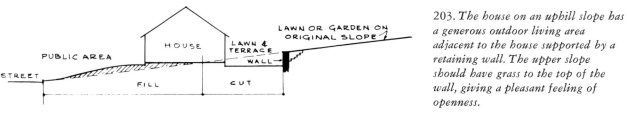

HOUSE · ORIGINAL SLOPE · WALL · WALL · ORIGINAL SLOPE · FILL · CUT

204. *A cross slope can be made more usable by grading it into a relatively level outdoor living area related to the house.*

205

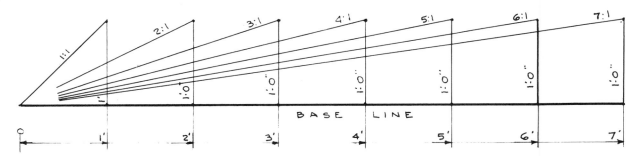

205. A composite diagram illustrating
some of the common slopes or
gradients used in the landscape.

206. Here a retaining wall was built
because there was an abrupt change of
grade. As this lawn area is off the
living room, the wall also keeps guests
206 from slipping down the embankment.

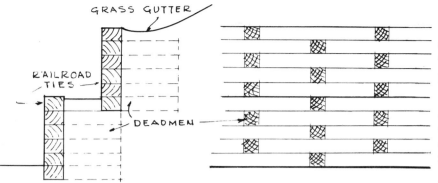

GRASS GUTTER

RAILROAD TIES

DEADMEN

SECTION   ELEVATION

207. *Railroad ties can be used to support steep slopes. Those illustrated are 2 feet 6 inches high with a grass gutter at the top to carry away runoff. Ties are spiked together; at each joint between ties a deadman (a railroad tie serving as brace) should be placed at right angles, extending into the bank, to anchor the wall. Shrubs may be planted to add interest.*

208. *Steep slopes should be planted in tough ground cover.*

14

CIRCULATION: GETTING AROUND

The landscape features useful for moving about by foot or car are practically universal but are often installed in haste and with little foresight. They deserve more careful design, for walks, paths and driveways serve a useful and psychological function. From the practical point of view, people and equipment should be able to move about safely and easily. The elements of circulation should be attractive, perhaps adding a note of mystery as to what lies beyond the graceful curve of a walk or drive—a half-hidden nook begging to be explored, a secret path which seems to disappear—these elements of the unexpected add charm and interest to the home landscape.

Features of circulation are also devices for organizing outdoor space. As the skeleton of a design, walks contribute character as well as form, dividing spaces into logical units forming a distinctive pattern. However, a circulation system should have a logical beginning; it should go where people wish to go, include points of interest, and eventually return to the house. There should be no dead ends. Thus walks and paths are secondary—after the basic outdoor spaces are organized, connect and/or separate them with walks and paths.

WALKS AND PATHS

Although good walks proceed in a straightforward manner, they need not be straight. Some of the most delightful walkways are designed in gentle flowing curves that move easily over the surface: beware, however, of walks that wiggle aimlessly. The artificially contorted walks of early suburbia were forced, impractical and unaesthetic. (For suggestions on the design of curved walks refer to Chapter 12.)

Straight paths usually look best on small plots. Sometimes a long straight path helps give a feeling of perspective, but it can also be monotonous. Here is an opportunity to introduce a feature or a series of related features, rhythmically placed.

Most American gardens have hopelessly skimpy paths; in fact they can seldom be made too wide. Even secondary paths should be at least *209*

4 feet wide—when edging plants overhang them, every inch is needed to accommodate two people walking abreast, the pleasantest way to share a garden. The main walk may be 5 or 6 feet wide, especially if it is grass. Sizeable garden beds need internal work paths at least 18 inches wide so the gardener may tend the plants without undue reaching. Elsewhere on the home landscape a path 8 feet wide will provide vehicular access, often a labor-saving item.

Since circulation also serves an aesthetic need, pattern alone may justify the building of a walk to enclose a grass panel, separate a flower bed from the lawn or set off a bit of garden architecture. The color and texture plus good line and proper proportion can make it a lovely asset not only as a foil for beds and borders, but also a frame giving depth and coherence to the composition.

There is abundant information available on materials and construction, and only a few general suggestions will be made here. It is important to use the right path in the right place. The ideal path is probably of beautiful, restful close-cut turf, in harmony with most places, large or small, formal or informal. (Besides, errors in design and proportion are never as apparent in grass as in paving.) However, a complete system of grass paths may be monotonous and is certainly impractical since it is usable only in dry weather. Grass also suffers under hard usage.

The simple gardens of colonial days often made use of gravel paths. They are equally useful today, but their success depends upon the same careful construction that goes into a tennis court, with no pebbles larger than half an inch in diameter. The modern version is often made of crushed stone or coarse gravel the size of a hen's egg, which not only makes the path unattractive but makes walking a real hazard. Paths of gravel and turf have more form and are easier to maintain if they are crowned (slightly higher in the center) to improve drainage, and edged with a curb. Woodland and wild garden paths can be informal with a surface of pine needles, tanbark, wood chips, pecan hulls, or a mix of fine gravel, coarse sand and a bit of oak-leaf mold.

Each property has everyday routes that must provide for all-weather traffic: from street to house, auto court to front entrance, from car to back door, kitchen door to garbage bins; from house to terrace, and in some gardening families, from house to garden. Muddy-shoe gardening can be avoided by cultivating beds on each side of an all-weather walk, such as one to the tool shed. All-weather walks should dry as soon as the rain stops and the sun appears. This means a good drainage base and proper pitch of ¼-inch per foot so water does not stand on the surface. Walks hit by the winter sun will be free of ice and snow sooner than shaded walks.

Gardens with formal patterns and structural features such as pools require neat paved stone or brick walks, laid dry on tamped sand or rockdust or on a more permanent concrete base. Joints should be tight and brushed with sand—avoid thyme or grass between stones for both safety and maintenance reasons. Brick is especially attractive as paving; its soft texture and interesting pattern blend well with lawn and plants. Concrete is a good utility material for service walks to kitchen, laundry, garbage platforms or garage court, where it may double as a skating rink or bicycle area. Tinted concrete or concrete paving with an exposed aggregate or brushed surface may be admitted to the garden. Stepping stones set on sand with grass between can be used for occasional inconspicuous paths. Stones should be a scant inch above soil level, so they can be overlapped by the lawn mower. Individual stones may be 18 or 20 inches square, and should be set to measure 2 feet from center to center. Stones are often installed on 3-foot centers, but they are too far apart for all but tall people.

Ideally, walks and paths should be no steeper than 5 per cent—5 feet of drop in 100 feet of horizontal run. (See Chapter 13.) Walks steeper than 6 per cent are hazardous under icy conditions. Utility walks may be as steep as 8 per cent, and occasionally it may be necessary to increase the slope to 12 per cent for a short distance. On steep terrain a series of stepped ramps may sometimes be used. (See Drawing 220.) A half-buried railroad tie or locust post held in place by long stakes or iron pins will form the riser or step-up. This should be no more than 6 inches high. The ramp or tread between risers works best if it measures 6 feet 6 inches from one riser to the next. It should pitch enough to drain, and it may pitch as much as 6 per cent if necessary. Each ramp will be just the right length for left and right foot to alternate in traveling up or down. (It is tiring when one foot must continuously repeat the same motion without relief.)

Whether changes of grade exist naturally or are contrived, one must provide steps for comfort and convenience in traveling from one level to another. Steps are delightful accessories in the garden, essentially utilitarian but with great aesthetic possibilities. A difference of levels arouses interest, and steps carefully placed and designed beckon the viewer with a gentle invitation to investigate what lies beyond.

STEPS

Garden steps must have simplicity, good proportion, form and line, and a harmonious relation to the setting. Formal steps of cut stone are out of place on a woodland path, and rough fieldstone is inappropriate for a Georgian residence. Both design and construction materials must reflect, enhance and harmonize with the scene.

The scale of many outdoor features is largely a matter of good taste or judgment. Steps are an exception because they are related to the human leg—if steps cannot be easily negotiated, they are out of scale. There is a subtle, often underestimated, difference between interior and exterior steps. Indoors, where space is sometimes minimal and stairs must reach from one floor to the next, a tight relation of tread and riser is common. ("Tread" is the flat surface that accommodates the foot; "riser" is the vertical space between treads.) Indoor treads are usually less than 12 inches wide, and risers higher than 6 inches. Outdoor space is less confining, and exterior steps may have a relaxed no-hurry feeling in keeping with the landscape. Outdoor treads should be wider and risers less steep than those indoors, unless there is no alternative. Recent tests on the design of stairs for safety and economy of effort suggest that no riser should be less than 4 inches nor more than 7 inches high. Treads should be at least 11 inches deep, but no deeper than 14 inches. (See Drawing 223.)

Select the combination that best fits the slope and landscape setting. There should be no deviation within the flight of steps from the chosen ratio—changing the height of a single riser may result in an accident because the climber's rhythmic pattern is broken. This applies not only to a single flight but to succeeding flights if they are close together. Proper relation of riser and tread determines the safety and comfort of outdoor steps.

Some thought should be given to the third dimension—the width of the flight. Good outdoor scale suggests that exterior steps be wider than those indoor because of the more expansive setting. Four feet 6 inches should be the minimum width, and 5 or 6 feet may be in better scale in many situations. A delightful effect can be achieved by using three well-designed steps offering generously wide, easy access from one level to a slightly higher one beyond. A minor change of grade can certainly be handled by a slope, but a wide flight of easy steps adds grace and rhythmic beauty. A single step in an unexpected spot along a much-traveled main walk can be dangerous if there is no apparent reason for it, but an occasional step or two in the garden may be introduced to add interest. Native weathered stone is the most charming material for a step which may be draped with a bit of spreading cotoneaster and have mossy joints.

There are situations where grass steps may be used if traffic is not overly heavy. These should be wide enough to accommodate the lawn mower—20 inches would do nicely, used with a 4-inch brick riser. For easy maintenance the grass tread should be enclosed on all four sides with a brick mowing strip.

All steps start at one level and end at a higher elevation. Some climb directly, while others curve gently or travel in a tight spiral. Still others move up to a landing, reverse direction and continue climbing. The site and the wishes of the owner will influence the design. Five or 6 steps in a run with a landing several paces long may be repeated several times and still not discourage the climber, since he can always see a break ahead. Steps leading from an upper walk down onto a terrace may flare out to suggest a generous transition from a smaller to a larger space. Wing walls are used for safety and appearance on each side of a flight of steps, supporting the soil at the upper level and keeping it from washing onto the steps; on a steep climb, balusters should be added. In designing curved or circular steps, the proper ratio of tread and riser should be used along the "line of travel" where most people will walk, usually about 18 inches out from the handrail. Recessed lights can be incorporated in the check-walls for night safety.

GETTING AROUND BY CAR

The most conspicuous item of circulation is easily the vehicular driveway and parking area already considered in Chapter 4. This is a highly visible, heavily used and most expensive outdoor feature, and it deserves correct construction for a long life-span. If there is room for off-the-street parking, and backing out is not necessary, a delightful drive is often possible with just enough curve to add charm and perhaps a degree of privacy from the street. (The alignment of driveway curves is amply covered in Chapter 12.) Roads and drives should be crowned or pitched for quick drainage, and a horizontal slope of 2 to 3 per cent on the drive will move water away from the house and parking area. If there is a change of grade between house and street, the profile should follow an ogee curve—a long gentle vertical curve at the entrance from the street and again at the top as the drive levels off at the auto court, garage and parking area, with a short straight run connecting them. On steep terrain a long horizontally curved driveway may be required to reduce the steepness encountered on a more direct route.

209. *Walks should be designed to take you where you want to go easily.*

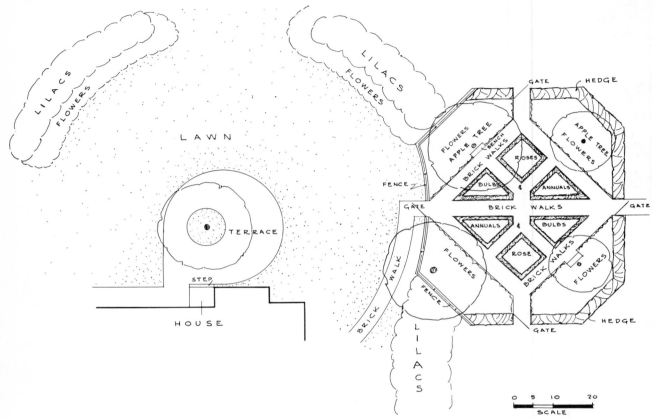

The labels in the diagram include:

LILACS, FLOWERS, LILACS, FLOWERS, LAWN, TERRACE, STEP, HOUSE, GATE, HEDGE, FLOWERS, APPLE TREE, BENCH, APPLE TREE, FLOWERS, BRICK WALKS, ROSES, FENCE, BULBS, ANNUALS, GATE, BRICK WALKS, GATE, BRICK WALK, ANNUALS, BULBS, FLOWERS, ROSE, BRICK WALKS, FLOWERS, FENCE, LILACS, GATE, HEDGE

0 5 10 20
SCALE

210. *This small garden uses brick walks as an important design
element, forming a pattern of small boxwood-bordered beds
which contain roses and bulbs followed by annuals. Apple tree
beds contain perennials. The fence curves to blend with a simple
circular lawn area surrounding a paved terrace under a maple.
A curved walk leads from garden to entrance.*

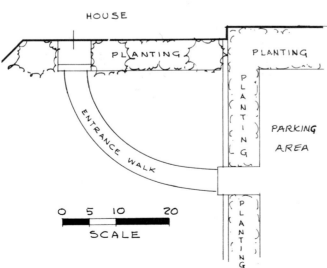

HOUSE

PLANTING

PLANTING

P L A N T I N G

ENTRANCE WALK

PARKING AREA

0 5 10 20

SCALE

P L A N T I N G

211. *Space should first be organized logically and then separated or connected with walks. In this way you have a smooth circulation system around your property.*

212. *Curved walks are sometimes used inappropriately, but this is one instance where a curve is both practical and attractive.*

213. *A harmonious path of grass.*

214. *Long walks need something to break the monotony—in this case, a rhythmic planting of crab apple trees on either side.*

216. *Woodland paths are informal. Many different materials can be used such as pine needles and ground corn cobs, shown here. Quietness adds to the charm.*

215. *Gravel paths such as this one are both durable and unobtrusive.*

217. *Formal gardens require paved walks of neat stone or brick.*

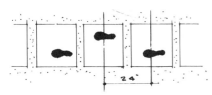

218. *When laying out stepping-stone paths in a long gentle curve, carefully stake out the center line before placing the stones.*

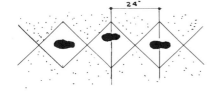

219. *A pleasant variation of usual stepping-stone pattern uses 18 inch square stones with corners touching and forming the center line.*

220. *Stepped ramps are useful where the grade is not steep enough for a flight of steps yet too steep for a sloping path.*

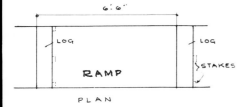

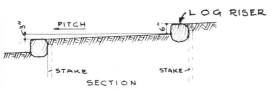

STEPPED RAMP

221. *Steps are one of the most delightful accessories. This stone walk up to a swimming pool was carefully worked out so that the flat area or ramp takes three average steps. The steps up, or risers, take three more, so that left and right alternate without a break when stepping up.*

222. *These garden steps meet good design qualifications.*

223. *Four ratios of tread and riser for use on outdoor steps are illustrated here.*

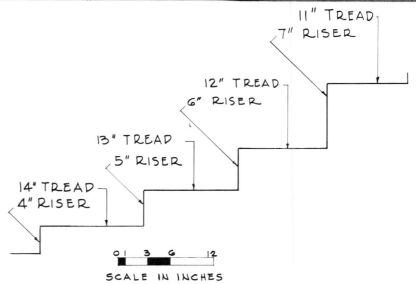

11" TREAD
7" RISER

12" TREAD
6" RISER

13" TREAD
5" RISER

14" TREAD
4" RISER

0 1   3   6   12
SCALE IN INCHES

224. *These steps have an unusual form because they join a circular grass panel and a curved brick walk.*

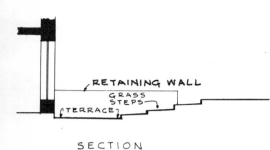

SECTION

RETAINING WALL

GRASS STEPS

TERRACE

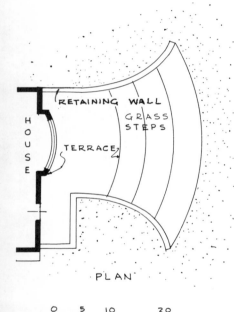

RETAINING WALL

GRASS STEPS

HOUSE

TERRACE

PLAN

0   5   10   20

SCALE

225. *A small brick terrace outside an English basement garden room was intimately connected to the lawn and garden at a higher level by ramped grass steps supported by brick risers. Retaining walls at each side swing out to suggest a gracious ascent. (See photograph at right.)*

226. *A partial view of the wide grass steps taken from the terrace.*

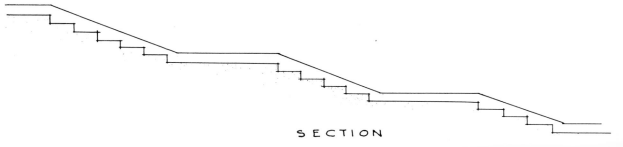

SECTION

ALL STEPS: 5" RISER & 15" TREAD

CHEEK WALL

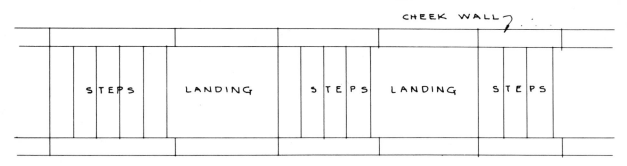

STEPS | LANDING | STEPS | LANDING | STEPS

PLAN

227. *A long run of steps is more inviting if broken into several small flights alternating with landings.*

225

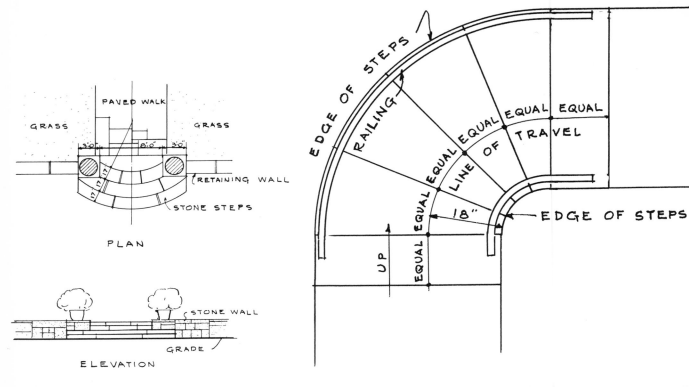

GRASS   PAVED WALK   GRASS

3'0"   8'0"   3'0"

17   17

17

RETAINING WALL

STONE STEPS

PLAN

STONE WALL

GRADE

ELEVATION

EDGE OF STEPS

RAILING

EQUAL EQUAL EQUAL EQUAL EQUAL

LINE OF TRAVEL

EQUAL EQUAL

18"

EDGE OF STEPS

UP

228. *When a walk and steps lead to a terrace or lawn at a lower level, a pleasant effect is achieved if they curve gently forward, suggesting a generous feeling of space.*

229 (top right). *With circular stairs, the width of the tread is narrower at the center and wider at the outer edge.*

230 (right). *A path which flares out indicates a transition from a walk into a larger area.*

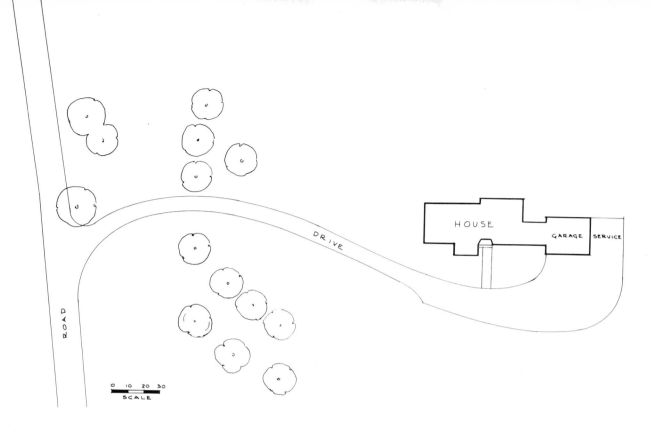

HOUSE

GARAGE | SERVICE

DRIVE

ROAD

0 10 20 30
SCALE

231. *A gentle flowing curve makes an attractive private drive.*

232. *The ogee curve, composed of two vertical curves joined together by a short straight line or tangent, is a perfect profile for a sloping driveway joining a house and a street. The long gentle curves at the top and bottom allow the car to level off before turning into the street or entering the garage. The steepest part of the profile occurs along the straightaway portion of the drive.*

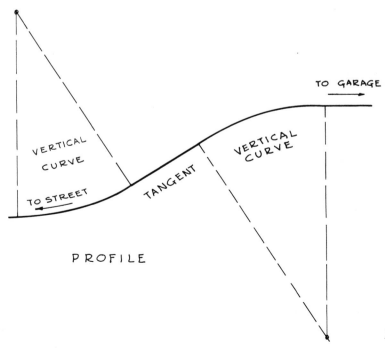

TO GARAGE

VERTICAL CURVE

TO STREET

TANGENT

VERTICAL CURVE

PROFILE

227

15

ACCENTS AND FEATURES IN THE LANDSCAPE

Emphasis on everything is emphasis on nothing. An artist composes a picture within the limits of his canvas while emphasizing the important part in one or more ways. He may give it an important position, making it the focus in the same way a colonial church spire dominates a New England village scene. He may use lines or a series of small accents leading the eye to the center of interest. He may use contrast of light and dark, or lead the eye to the focal point by a sequence or gradation of light and dark.

The well-designed landscape begins with a unified composition embodying the principles of simplicity, good scale, balance, sequence and focus; each unit of the whole must also embody these principles. Features of interest that enrich and embellish the landscape scene make attractive focal points in the garden.

Balance is very important here. Formal gardens are symmetrically balanced with the attractions on one side of the center line equal to the attractions on the opposite side. In asymmetrical balance the sum of the attractions on one side is equal to the sum of the attractions on the other, even though the two sides are not alike. Japanese prints and gardens are perfect examples of this. Nature's compositions are full of variety and are almost never symmetrical, yet they satisfy due to their inherent balance.

The day of the large formal garden is almost past, but there are still opportunities for small symmetrical gardens with pattern beds arranged along a central axis with an appropriate feature at the end. This may be as simple as a well-designed gate terminating the center path. Square or circular gardens may also have a central motif, with beds of equal size divided by two walks intersecting at right angles. Their cross axis may be marked by something as unobtrusive as a millstone; a sundial, bird bath, pool or dipping well can also serve as the feature as long as it is below eye level and in scale and character with the garden. A central motif can also be achieved with an appropriate paving pattern at the cross axis. The focal point need not be conspicuous; it may *229* add no more than a touch of whimsy, a decorative note, a bit of color or an interesting form to the design.

Minor accents in the garden or terrace can be accomplished by vases, urns, clipped topiary and plants in containers, dominating less important parts of the picture. They may mark the corners of a glass plot or flower bed, defining the shapes and giving them importance. Matched features each side of a gate will also do this, and two features at opposite ends of a garden will call attention to a center line even if it is not marked by a path.

A neat, well formed garden with organized flower beds is a focal point in the landscape. On a smaller scale flowers and plants make endlessly decorative features on the terrace, on a wall or parapet, on the sides of steps, as rhythmic notes around the swimming pool, and in countless spots where some colorful note would be welcome. Interesting containers enhance their decorative value.

Such features need not be limited to the garden proper. An architectural note is often a welcome relief in a sea of green foliage, and a well-chosen feature can transform a lawn and give it genuine interest. An outdoor feature must be carefully weighed for scale and balance. Is it too small or too large for the space? Too light or too heavy? Too delicate, too crude or casual for the setting? Will it seem to belong where it is placed? Would there be a sense of loss if it were taken away?

With careful planning, small buildings may be used as landscape features. A tool house, garden shelter, or gazebo may be just right at the end of the garden. A pool house and terrace may dominate a side lawn used for recreation. A shed for mower and snow plow can crown a gentle slope in the meadow, and the children's playhouse may serve as a focal feature in the play yard.

Garden benches have been widely used as terminal features. However, benches should be placed in spots where they can be used as well as seen. A comfortable wooden seat with back and arm rests located under an old apple tree is much more effective and useful than a backless white stone bench in the blazing noonday sun. Why not have several tucked away in various spots—one for birdwatching, another in a spot bathed by early morning light, a third for watching evening constellations.

Sculpture is art's great contribution to the landscape. An amalgam of architectural forms plus a suggestion of a living thing, it is a representation rather than an imitation. Here, too, scale is an important consideration. Outdoor objects must be larger than interior features of similar nature or they will seem too small and out of scale. A feature is out of scale if it makes everything else in the garden look too large or too small. A statue should be separated from its setting by a pedestal or base so that it looks like a statue. Sun and shadow give modeling and a three-dimensional aspect. Statues with one face make excellent terminal features. They may be placed against a background of planting or construction—a wall, fence or building, or in niches of planting or masonry. Statues in the round or with more than one face may be used at the intersection of two axes, real or assumed. Others may stand free, silhouetted against the sky or the distant landscape. Some may be set in the open, to be viewed from all sides, preempting the surrounding lawn space. Some are prima donnas dominating their setting; some may compete or cooperate with architecture or plant forms; others are quiet and unobtrusive and one may come upon them unexpectedly.

Finely detailed marble should be viewed close at hand in a sophisticated setting: well-groomed lawns and perhaps a clipped ever-green backdrop. A rough-hewn St. Francis would be at home under a native shadblow, and a stone rabbit beside a hedgerow. Casual settings can use bold incisive forms with strong silhouettes. Figures of bronze, lead, grey fiberglass or weathered stone look well in an informal landscape, and native stone may serve as a base. Driftwood and unusual rock formations also make good accents. In places where bedrock lies at or near the surface, natural ledges can be exposed and treated as a sculptured form in its own right, or serve as a base for other features.

The Orientals excel in the artistic and symbolic use of rocks as sculptural forms. The many superb rock formations are undervalued in this country; to us they are just rocks.

Trees too may be treated as sculpture. The remnants of a venerable oak may dominate a knoll. Weeping forms and cut-leaved varieties also serve to accent space. Weeping evergreens may cascade down a slope, or a Japanese maple provide color accent. A single tree of usual form or color is not always interesting enough to serve as focal point. A better arrangement is to combine a shelter or a seat with a tree or two for silhouette and shadow pattern.

A view of a hill or valley, a church steeple, a pond or brook, a picturesque freestanding tree or an appropriate building is also a welcome addition to the informal landscape composition. Develop any views that can be included in the picture. Often plants can be added or removed to give framing on either side. Lines of boundary planting should help to carry the eye toward the feature in the distance.

In arid countries water is the lifeblood of the garden. Water features are widely used and appreciated in many parts of the world though seldom with the same artistry and effectiveness as in the Islamic gardens of Spain, where water makes the garden. In more humid climates water shares the limelight with plants and other features. (See Photograph 244 and Drawing 245.) Some lucky places have views of natural water features. The Japanese have excelled at creating the illusion of water where none exists. Thanks to plastic tubing and the recirculating pump, most gardens or terraces may have some type of water feature as a focal point. The range is extensive, from the simplest of birdbaths in the backyard to the ultimate—a wall formed by a sheet of falling water at the rear of a small public garden, such as one finds in New York City.

Still water in the garden suggests quietude and reflection; moving water is laughing water, a combination of sound and motion. Large or deep pools with dark linings are best for still water, while water from jet, splash or waterfall is more effective in shallow basins with light linings. Color can be added through the use of glazed tile in basin, coping, or wall plaques. Foliage in colorful containers can give line, texture and mass to the composition.

Terrace and garden furnishings serve double duty—they are for use and embellishment. A terrace designed as foreground or setting for a house may need little or no decoration, but a terrace planned for use is incomplete without comfortable accessories for sitting, lounging, eating and relaxing. If these furnishings add color, warmth and interest, they will be decorative features as well.

233. Well-integrated accessories are an important part of landscape design.

Fire on a patio or terrace easily becomes a focus for social activities. A grill may be a neat permanent construction built into the side of the house, making use of a house chimney, surrounded by paving and protected by an overhanging roof. Less elaborate are portable wheeled grills, braziers and barbecues. A circular pit lined with brick and equipped with a grate and solid cover is simple and unobtrusive in terrace or lawn, yet large enough to roast a whole lamb. A permanent outdoor fireplace of fieldstone or brick is less useful than moveable equipment. An elaborate masonry barbecue-fireplace in the garden is often overpowering in scale and too conspicuous the year round to be worthwhile in any setting except perhaps in California.

234. A cross axis in this herb garden features a rustic sundial grounded in a bed of thyme.

235 (right). *Yet another plant feature is this topiary duck. Not a simple matter to achieve, but what fun.*

236 (below). *An attractive lath house forms a background for a formal herb garden.*

237. *Minor accents can also be achieved by plant material. This boxwood trained as a standard with a small curved hedge leads the way to a formal flower garden.*

238. *Bold black iron steps, more for show than use, offset the texture of a wisteria vine against a white wall.*

239. *Objects from abroad are favorite garden accessories. A pool from Spain is a focus here. Such a feature must be carefully considered.*

240. *Garden seats and benches are favorite accessories and terminal features.*

241. *Appropriate sculpture in proper scale always adds interest.*

242. *At the end of a formal terrace a sculptured fountain is pleasing and refreshing.*

243 (right). *In an informal landscape native stone may serve as a base or background feature.*

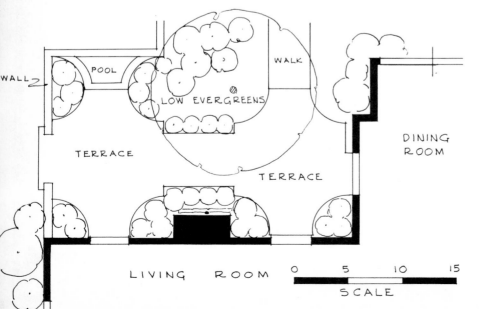

244 and 245 (above and left).
*Garden pools come to us from the
arid countries where water is the
lifeblood of the garden—a cooling
agent for body and spirit—like this
pool and fountain on a paved terrace.*

WALL

POOL

WALK

LOW EVERGREENS

TERRACE

TERRACE

DINING ROOM

LIVING ROOM

SCALE

0   5   10   15

246 (right). *What is more delightful
than the soft tinkling of a windbell?*

16

TOWARD A MORE
PLEASANT
PRIVATE CLIMATE

Although Mark Twain complained that everyone talked about the weather but did nothing about it, man has unfortunately been doing something about it for quite some time. He has made significant changes in his physical environment, many of which make the world less attractive, less healthy and less comfortable to live in. Mismanagement of agricultural lands resulted in the Dust Bowl; uncontrolled industrialization has created widespread pollution and the energy crisis. Many of these environmental changes affect the local climate, usually adversely.

The soil under its mulch of leaves on the oak forest floor does not get very cold in winter nor very hot in summer. But let the trees be cut down, ridges bulldozed, swamps filled and a development installed —with streets, driveways, houses and acres of paved parking for shopping centers—and the mild climate of the oak forest becomes a man-made climate not unlike the desert: hot in summer, cold in winter. There are few climate-tempering devices to compare with the forest. During summer, the understory may be as much as 25 degrees cooler than the canopy, and winter lows are never as extreme as those in the open land. There is far greater retention of ground water in the forest as opposed to grassland or bare soil, since the shade of trees overhead greatly reduces evaporation. Temperature and humidity vary from layer to layer, with temperatures highest in the canopy and humidity highest on the forest floor. The refreshing coolness of the woodlands is a pleasant respite from open, sun-swept areas.

On the home grounds, a similar relation between open spaces and woods can be employed on a smaller scale. Every house and garden, however small, has more than one climate. There is a world of difference between the sheltered southeast angle of the house and the cold, shady northwest corner. These represent microclimates. Some are a result of the house layout and its location on the site; others are inherent in the land itself. Little can be done about changing an existing house location, and only a limited number of changes can be made in the 243 topography of a small property. However, one's private climate, within its limited area, may be modified by the careful placement of wisely selected plants, making it more liveable and usable than the local climate.

Abundant sunshine makes for happier, healthier people and gardens, and fortunate indeed is the homeowner whose house and land receive a bountiful supply. Even in winter it warms the skier by instantaneous radiant heat (such as that from an electric heater) which, together with light, makes up the radiant energy of the sun. It warms one indoors as it streams through a sunny window, also warming the walls and floors, which in turn warm the air, raising the interior temperature and reducing fuel bills. (See Chapter 3.)

In July, when high temperatures add up to considerable discomfort, one must do something about solar radiation, air circulation and humidity. A good place to begin is by providing some form of shade. Bare ground surfaces in the Imperial Valley registering temperatures up to 152 degrees in the sun dropped an average of 32 degrees five minutes after shade covered the ground.

There are many man-made shading devices—the umbrella, awning, canopy, arbor, sunscreen, lattice, egg-crate and louver, to name a few. Better still is shade from deciduous trees or vines, nature's automatic sunshades. Accurate placement of plants is all the homeowner needs to profit from this built-in heat control system.

In contrast to man-made shading devices, the tree's thin leaves are aligned so that a maximum of leaf surface is turned toward the sun; this results in maximum shade coupled with an abundance of open spaces for air circulation. Leaves are bathed in moisture drawn up from the earth and evaporated as a by-product of photosynthesis. This process cools the leaf, which then cools the air around it—living leaves are only 5 to 10 degrees warmer than the air on a sunny summer day. When a slight breeze is blowing, the air temperature under the tree may register 10 to 15 degrees less than the temperature outside the tree canopy. The cool air gradually moves downward, cooling all who sit beneath it. As the sun sets, the surrounding warm air rises and is replaced by cool air moving in from a layer close to the ground. Under a tree's broad canopy, the slow upward movement of warm air may be trapped during the early evening hours. Thus the tree may provide a tent of warm air on a cool summer evening.

Plants also naturally help to reduce pollution. Bad air is diluted and enriched with oxygen-laden air in and around the leaves. Stems, branches and leaves serve as a grid in removing particulate pollutants, trapping them by tiny hairs and moisture particles, later washed away by rain. In calm wooded areas other particles settle to the ground as the wind velocity is reduced, while moisture given off by plants cleans the dusty air.

If trees are to help control climate in winter and sumer they must be placed carefully to take full advantage of the sun's angle and seasonal direction. Since winter sun adds comfort to the house thermally and psychologically, deciduous shade trees must be used in the house area. Medium-sized varieties which attain a 40-foot height and spread at maturity are preferred for the average house. If the house faces south (with a south terrace as well), a tree should be placed at the southwest corner. Here it would cast no shade on the terrace in the morning when the sun is usually welcome. By late morning and early afternoon it will shade part of the terrace, some of the roof and south wall. It will give the greatest shade by mid-afternoon. By late afternoon the south wall, roof and terrace will be shaded by the house itself.

Trees southwest of the terrace and house may well be the most important on the small property, and should be chosen with an eye to maximum effect. This is the place to invest in a good nursery-grown balled and burlapped tree of enough height and spread to start paying its way immediately. If a limited amount of money is available, spend it on the lawn and on one or two good shade trees for the southwest and west. The rest can wait.

Another type of solar heat comes from the low afternoon sun. Contrary to popular opinion, it is the west, and not the south side of the house which is hottest in summer. The problem of keeping summer sun from shining into south windows is easily solved by proper over-hang, or an eyebrow, but these cannot protect west or northwest windows because of the sun's low, almost horizontal, angle. A tall vertical screen to the west and northwest is one solution, but it will also cut off any view. If views are important, use a moveable vertical screen or a vertical awning during June, July and August afternoons. Or you might use a series of baffles of fencing, clipped hedge or a trellis with deciduous vines, to intercept the sun's rays. A row of tall growing shrubs or small flowering trees across the west side of the house and extending beyond both corners not only keeps the low afternoon sun out, but more important, it keeps it off the west and north walls. The tallest tree should be toward the southwest, and placed 20 to 25 feet from the corner. The tree on the northwest should be shortest, to take into account the lowered angle of the setting sun. Trees on the west should also be low-branched with dense heads for the same reason. This is a fine spot for crabapples or hawthorne, dogwood, and similar short-trunked flowering trees.

Other types of planting may be used if trees can't be grown due to shallow soil or lack of space. House walls and paved terraces can often be shaded by vines supported on an overhead arbor. A south window can be shaded by a narrow trellis above it, supporting a deciduous vine. Masonry walls would profit from a green covering of self-clinging vines, especially on the west. Walls of wood or aluminum siding may be shaded by vines grown on vertical supports in front of them; these would also cool by evaporation in the air space between foliage and house. Walls may also be screened by high shrub masses planted in front of them.

A warm dry layer of air lies above dry bare soil or paving, but a cool moist layer of air lies above grass. When grass or ground cover extend up to the house wall, this layer of heavier cool air can be brought into the house through low openings; if high openings are used on an opposite wall, true cross-ventilation will be achieved. A planting of low shrubs against the house wall would produce the same result and keep the soil even cooler. Cool air can be taken in at night by fans through basement windows or a sunken terrace.

Plants and trees provide yet another service by reducing the discomfort of glare from the sun or a spotlight at night. Reflection is daylight magnified and bounced off bright polished surfaces such as glass or water and it can be equally uncomfortable. A whitish hazy summer sky gives off the fiercest glare of all, second only to the sun. Shade trees close to the house cut out the glary sky and sun, but let in, under the canopy of leaves, the view of the indirectly lighted general landscape so pleasant to the eye. Modern glass-walled houses may use glare-proof glass or a green overhang made of regularly spaced dense-foliaged trees clipped to form a green awning extending from the eaves. Plants can reduce reflections if they are placed where they can intercept light before it hits the reflecting surface. The closer the plant to the source of light, the better it performs. Usually it is easier to screen out reflected light before it reaches the viewer. Trees, shrubs, grass and ground cover can be used. Even plants in containers help break up and soften glare and reflections from paved surfaces.

One's private climate is also made more pleasant by the use of plants as wind control devices. This may include deflecting, guiding, slowing, accelerating or stopping the air passage. An avenue of trees parallel to the prevailing summer winds can help channel and amplify the breeze. Beware, however, of blocking up the far end of the avenue or the cooling effect will be lost. Sometimes plantings can be designed to cool by increasing wind velocity. Breezes may be channeled through an opening in a heavily planted hedgerow or wind barrier so that the air flow is concentrated in a desired spot. Wind direction can also be guided by an angled mass of plant material.

Since prevailing winds usually shift directions with a change of season, the same evergreen screen planting may deflect the northwest winds around the house. Curved wind deflectors work better than straight ones which the wind hits head on. Here too, it is important to leave a place for the wind to go; don't dam up the flow.

Low temperatures and strong winds make for winter discomfort and anything that reduces winter wind velocity will make the house more comfortable and a garden less subject to winter damage. It takes more fuel to heat a house when the temperature is 32 degrees with a 12-mile wind than when the temperature is zero with a 3-mile wind. A house with high land to the north may be protected by a thick evergreen planting increasing in height from north to south so winter winds sweep up and over the top of the house. Thick belts of trees and shrubs can reduce wind velocity by 50 per cent for a distance downwind of ten times their height. Dense evergreen screen plantings are the most effective windbreaks. Trees gradually slow the wind, while letting some pass through. Groves of trees to windward give protection, and deciduous as well as evergreen plants are helpful here. Maximum protection is assured with a series of windbreaks, each acting like a baffle, eventually slowing the air to a near stand-still. If there is no room for a windbreak, use a tall, thin long wall or fence which should not be completely impenetrable, as openings help prevent air turbulence.

From the standpoint of a long gardening season, it is important to understand the principles of air drainage. Cool air flows slowly downhill like molasses and a slope no greater than 1 foot of drop in 100 feet of length is enough to insure this flow. If cool air can be collected and contained at a low spot it makes a delightful evening sitting area. A pool of water will further add to the coolness. A wall, tight fence or evergreen hedge can form the low side of this area, but anything blocking the air flow from above should be removed.

However, this cool summer area will be a frost pocket in spring and fall. Plants on top of the slope may be safe while those in the low spots suffer frost damage. This can be prevented in several ways. Sometimes the cold air can be made to flow around the garden. Or use a dam on the uphill side to keep cold air from moving down. A 1-foot fence or wall may be enough as the cold air layer is only a few inches thick; a low evergreen hedge is almost as good as a wall. If there is a gate or an opening at the lowest point of the property, the cold air will flow out through it, traveling further downhill and sparing damage to the garden. An enclosed garden will often escape the first frost if a tree with a good canopy is growing in the center. Warm daytime air will be trapped under it and may be enough to counter the frost.

Bright sunny windy weather of spring and fall can be enjoyed if one can sit protected from the wind. An inside corner of the house, open to the south and east, can be developed into a sun trap. Light-colored walls will reflect the sun's heat; a small paved area of light bluestone will absorb it. Such an area can be dry and snow-free while less protected spots lie under a blanket of snow. In early spring when

247. Every house and garden has to contend with the seasonal conditions existing in its particular setting.

the temperature in the wind reads 52 degrees, the thermometer in the sunspot may register 80 to 90 degrees. Such a protected spot can add up to three extra months of outdoor use. Even in mid-winter there will be days allowing for basking in the sun.

Noise is an increasing problem everywhere and the homeowner often has little control over it, especially if it comes from street traffic or planes. Unfortunately, on a small property not much relief is available. Freestanding walls and tight fences covered with dense vines are sound-absorbing to some degree. Dense hedges at least 2 feet thick can reduce the noise level by 4 to 5 decibels. Where space is available earth berms or mounds are helpful, especially if covered with dense planting. A 6-foot berm topped with a dense hedge at least 4 feet high should reduce traffic noises by 8 decibels. In general, noise control requires dense planting of considerable depth and height to achieve a reasonable amount of sound insulation.

248. One's private climate may be modified within limits by the wise choice and placement of plants. Here a sophisticated treatment of a pin oak tree serves as an umbrella, shading the side entrance to the house and part of the terrace.

249. *This porch-terrace with its open vine-covered overhead structure filters the summer sun while letting in the winter sun.*

250. *A house with no trees or grass around it is fully exposed to the sun's rays which heat the roof and walls, the bare soil and the layers of air above them.*

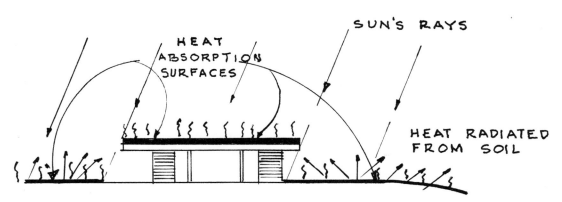

SUN'S RAYS

HEAT ABSORPTION SURFACES

HEAT RADIATED FROM SOIL

251

251. *A tea-wing is a whimsical name for this shaded arbor. Cool breezes flow freely. Leaves and grass absorb some of the heat. When the temperature soars, iced tea with friends requires no air-conditioning for comfort here.*

252. *The house and its trees, shrubs, grass and a vine-covered arbor are all fully exposed to the sun. The resulting evaporation lowers the temperature of leaves and soil and creates a mass of cool moist air under and around plants, which helps to cool the house.*

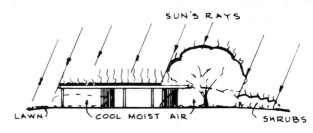

253. *Heat does not build up in leaves; they are natural air-conditioners.*

254. *The most important tree on the small property may be the one which shades the terrace. It should be placed on the southwest corner where it will provide enough shade for a luncheon table. A second tree off the southwest corner would cool the house as well.*

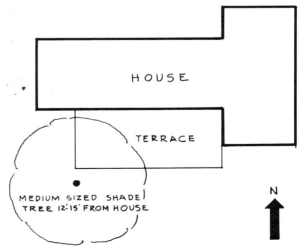

HOUSE

TERRACE

MEDIUM SIZED SHADE TREE 12-15' FROM HOUSE

N

255. *A well placed pin oak shades this paved terrace.*

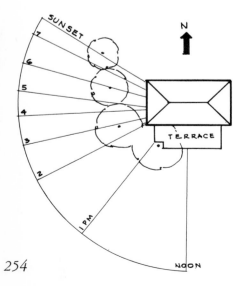

256. *Several trees are required to protect the west walls and windows from the afternoon sun and its heat.*

257. *Large maple trees shade this extended terrace on a sunny afternoon.*

258. *An "eyebrow" of grape, wisteria or other suitable vines helps relieve the summer glare from sun shining on large expanses of glass.*

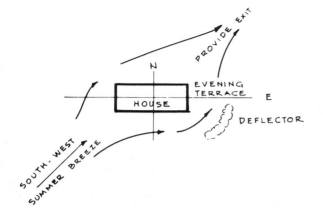

259. *Since the prevailing summer breeze is often from the south or southwest, a house on a south or southwest slope with no heavy planting to interrupt the movement of air should be blessed with good air circulation. A band of planting some distance off the southeast corner would help to channel the breeze and make for a cool east terrace. However, it is important to provide an air exit, hopefully to the northeast, so that the circulation continues.*

260. *A row of clipped linden trees acts as an awning against the glare on the porch and glass-walled living room.*

261. *Anything that can be done to reduce winter wind velocity will make the house more comfortable and do less damage to the garden. A hedge serves admirably.*

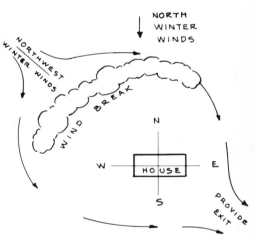

262. *North and northwest winter winds can be deflected around a house by curved plantings of thick hedges or evergreens. Again, it is important to provide an exit. Such a windbreak is helpful in winter but does not reduce the cooling effect of summer breezes.*

263. *A louvered panelled fence lets air through in the summer. The overhang of the house shields the windows from the overhead sun. The gravel courtyard, tastefully handled, is minimum maintenance itself.*

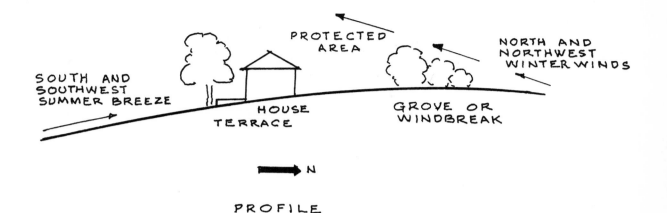

SOUTH AND SOUTHWEST SUMMER BREEZE

PROTECTED AREA

NORTH AND NORTHWEST WINTER WINDS

HOUSE TERRACE

GROVE OR WINDBREAK

N

PROFILE

264. Windbreaks of tall thick trees and evergreens reduce the wind velocity and make the house more comfortable in winter and the garden less subject to injury.

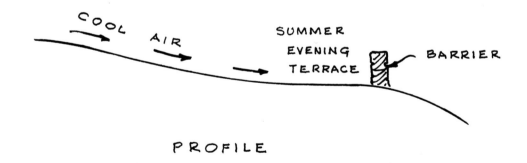

COOL AIR

SUMMER EVENING TERRACE

BARRIER

PROFILE

265. Since cool air flows downhill like molasses, if it can be collected and contained at a low point on the property that point can become a delightful spot for an evening sitting area.

17

LIGHTING
THE LANDSCAPE

Prometheus undoubtedly started outdoor lighting, but it did not catch on until the advent of picture windows allowing large views from our homes. By night these extensive glass areas become large black holes or black mirrors reflecting interior images and movement back into the house. The choice is between draping the glass or lighting the outdoor landscape. There is much to be said for the latter, and nowadays there is an increasing interest in the art of landscape illumination.

The aim of landscape illumination is to make the terrace and garden appear to be bathed in soft moonlight. It should illuminate interesting trees, silhouetting some and revealing the framework of others, creating shadow patterns of foliage and trunk. Pools of soft light should lead the eye along the walk in rhythmic sequence. Finally, the focal point should be accented in light from several sources, providing roundness and depth. Daylight comes from outer space and is profligate; garden lighting is internal and selective, aimed at achieving artistic effect. (It is the direct antithesis of lighting for security with its glaring spotlights revealing every garish detail.)

To accomplish such results requires imagination plus some amount of trial and error. Begin by taking inventory. What features are worth lighting? Will lighting be needed for walking, eating, sitting or working outdoors? Or will exterior effects be enjoyed only from within the house? Try to visualize how lighting will look when completed, then figure out how to accomplish the desired results.

The objective is to give darkness a touch of magic by the addition of the right kind of artificial light in the right place. Lights should not be features in themselves but devices to produce beauty at night. Light sources must be concealed; neither the light beam nor its origin should be apparent. Lights shining in the eyes of the beholder (or the next-door neighbor) defeat the whole effect. Avoid high intensity by using low-wattage bulbs. Lights of 150 watts or less are sufficient for most effects and clear white light is best. Light sources and fixtures must be equally unobtrusive by day. A plant in a grass area obviously installed to conceal a light fixture is usually worse than the fixture alone since it detracts from the simple uncluttered effect. Such fixtures may be concealed in a pipe below ground.

For the most natural effects, overhead light should originate from as high a source as possible; 16 feet is the minimum and 20 feet is preferable. (Lights at such heights also help to divert insects from the terrace.) Use a canister light or conceal the bulb in a slender metal tube so that the source can be seen only when standing directly beneath it. Lights may be placed in trees, on poles, on chimneys, or mounted high on the walls of buildings. Downlight is bounced upward as reflected diffused light which adds a pleasant glow to the surrounding darkness. Single lights should alternate with small clusters of lights to create varying soft patterns rather than uniform brightness over the large area. A group of two or three lights gives emphasis by the overlapping patterns. Some lights may be tilted 15 to 20 degrees to produce elliptical rather than circular patterns, thus suggesting progression along a walk or drive or down a garden path. Plants and flowers look most natural when lighted by white or blue-white light from above. Light filtering through tree or shrub foliage creates beautiful effects when arranged so that details of form and texture are transformed into shadow patterns. You can also use concealed lights in front of a planting to create dramatic patterns on walls or fences.

The portrait photographer achieves his effects by soft lighting plus one or two additional sources to bring out highlights, shadows and modeling. In the same manner accent light is added to garden moonglow for dramatic effect. But it must be handled with sensitivity and restraint; too often it is garish or overdone, destroying the subtle accentuation one hopes to achieve.

Accent lights usually originate from a point near the ground or below the surface. Sewer pipes make excellent containers for below-ground lights; they may also be concealed in shrubbery or shielded from view by special reflector hoods. These lights are projected upward,

266. *A pool in a natural setting reflects the artfully lighted tree trunks and foliage in the dark water.*

267. *Carefully concealed lighting in the crown of a palm tree adds an unusual effect of height to a garden and patio in Nassau.*

268. *A terrace at night is more restful with indirect lighting. Fixtures are recessed under the eaves.*

straight up to reveal the structure of a tree or unusual plant, or tilted at an angle to produce three-dimensional side-lighting and modeling. The best results are produced with two lights of different intensities at different angles. Sunset and sunrise effects are obtained by lighting large trees at a low angle, but the lights need to be well concealed by placing them at approximately a 60 degree angle. Recessed lights at the base of a building, fence or wall will make a finely-lighted background against which trees or plants may be silhouetted.

Outdoor terraces and patios are lighted in much the same way as the living room—soft light from high angles for general illumination plus local light as needed for cooking, eating and reading. Yellow lights are best here, as they do not attract insects. Additional downlighting on the terrace should be kept below eye level.

Light intensity may be built up at parking areas, entrance walks and steps to give a feeling of welcome and to prevent accidents. Well lights or visible fixtures may be used along a driveway or around an entrance court to define the edges and keep mediocre drivers out of the plantings. Moonlight effects from high sources can be supplemented by downlights below eye level to give pools of light. A series of small walkway lamps at sidewalk level will point the way, and recessed lights in cheek walls will illuminate steps. Small well-designed fixtures at regular intervals atop a low wall take the place of a safety railing and add a decorative feature as well.

Swimming pools are always lighted from under water. Garden pools are best when unlighted as they make delightful reflecting surfaces when the surrounding landscape is illuminated.

Planning for garden lighting should be done early. A landscape plan should show proposed exterior lighting so that cables and fixtures can be in place before the finished grading and planting are done. Use only approved waterproof cables, outlets, switches and fixtures.

18

SUGGESTIONS FOR MINIMUM MAINTENANCE

Contemporary landscapes can and should be planned for minimum maintenance, but not everyone has a newly-planned house and garden and those with older places are also concerned with the amount of time, energy and money that must go into upkeep. What can be done to ease the burden?

Overgrown shrubs and evergreens are the bane of many old places. Hedgerows and boundary plantings may be left undisturbed if space is not a problem; in fact, such spots make good bird cover. But old foundation plantings that interfere with light and air circulation should get the axe. Occasionally an old plant of special character may be pruned and kept to give scale, especially with a large or tall house. These oldtimers can be supplemented with a few new smaller-growing plants as required, but they should not create a new jungle. This new bed can be unified with appropriate ground cover bounded by a long flowing line and separated from the lawn by a mowing strip. (See Drawing 280.)

Big trees that overhang the roof, shutting out the sun, should be turned into firewood. Especially trying are big spruce or similar conifers that obstruct the sun all year round.

Many old places have large old-fashioned flower gardens or extensive perennial borders, often neglected and overgrown and too taxing for most homeowners to maintain. Still, many would be willing to keep the old gardens if they could be assets rather than liabilities. One way to accomplish this is to reduce the area planted in flowers. This reduction in cultivated space will ease the maintenance burden; it can be reduced even more by choosing only low-maintenance plants. (Consult *Saturday Morning Gardener* by Donald Wyman.) It may be possible to keep the same size and shape of bed or garden and replace a major portion of perennials with flowering shrubs and evergreens used as a frame, with accents and rhythmic notes lending form and mass. Large beds and borders can accommodate large plants and small flowering trees such as crabapple, dogwood and magnolias. Medium-sized gardens need less robust plants such as fragrant viburnum or shrub roses, while small beds can use dwarf shrubs or evergreens.

The whole area can be unified with an underplanting of ground cover that tolerates shade and the competition of shrub roots. Finally, a recurring pattern of cultivated spots containing favorite annuals, perennials and bulbs may be added along the sunny foreground of the redesigned garden. However, these are best separated from the surrounding ground cover areas by curbs or dividers of brick, sturdy aluminum, plastic or masonite strips, since most ground covers are aggressive and will give troublesome competition. Tulips can be interplanted with perennials and annuals, narcissus will compete successfully with newly planted ground cover, but bulbs added to established ground cover usually suffer.

A successful low-maintenance bed can be made by combining shrubs and easy-care perennials if shade-tolerant varieties of perennials are used. However, most perennials do better when they don't compete with shrub roots and overhanging branches. Even without herbaceous plants it is possible to have a flowering border of small trees, shrubs, broad-leaved evergreens and ground-cover plants if attention is given to succession of bloom. Furthermore, almost all plants require less care if they are mulched. This shades their roots, reduces loss of soil moisture, keeps down weeds and generally eliminates the need for edging and trimming.

In some gardens the center grass area may be enlarged to eliminate an area of flower border, as shown in Drawing 269.

Some places with extensive lawns are presently restricting them to neatly formed panels near the house and garden, while outlying portions are mowed less frequently and left to become sunny meadows. Property boundary plantings may be expanded with widely-spaced flowering trees, shrubs and evergreens, and the spaces between filled with ground cover, ferns, shade-tolerant wildflowers or some of the hosta varieties. Such a planting will soon become self-maintaining; it may add a new dimension to the property if a path of wood chips wanders through it.

In landscape as well as in other fields of design, beauty is often a by-product of efficiency. Lawns are easiest to maintain if they are simple compact shapes with easy flowing edges that lend themselves to the use of a power mower. Steep, narrow dead-end or hard-to-reach places should be taken out of grass and planted to shrubs or ground cover. Get rid of sharp corners and substitute sweeping curves which permit continuous instead of push-and-pull mowing.

If there are large areas of grass, keep a neat lawn around the house and treat the outlying areas as meadow, to be mowed once or twice a year to discourage brush and seedling trees. Woody plants may also be eliminated by spraying with brush killer. How does one treat the transition from mowed lawn to meadow? If the land falls away from the house in a slope the problem is easily solved—simply mow across the crest of the slope so that a clean line of mowed lawn is seen from the house. Or a low retaining wall can be used as transition, with lawn above and meadow below. If there is no appreciable change of grade, make the transition from lawn to meadow with a long, gently curving mow-line; this is much pleasanter than a lawn bounded by straight lines and corners.

Any grass area constantly worn thin by traffic should be replaced by some kind of paved walk or stepping stones. By the same token don't insist on trying to grow grass in impossible spots; the space beneath large Norway maples or beech trees is a good example. Decide where the lawn should end and install a mowing strip, using a good curved line to delineate the tree-controlled area. Gravel or bark mulch may be used under the tree but bear in mind that leaves must be raked up.

It is unrealistic to insist on a perfect green carpet unless the owner is a retired greensman. A lawn composed of several kinds of grass may not have the uniform texture of a putting green, but it will have fewer maladies. For a respectable lawn a routine schedule of feeding, mowing and watering may be necessary; however, proper planning can eliminate or greatly reduce trimming and edging where lawn meets buildings, walks, drives, terraces, flower borders, ground cover areas and shrub borders. Wherever possible, paved areas such as walks, drives, and terraces should be at the lawn level so the mower can overlap the paving and eliminate trimming. If raised curbs of granite block or heavy steel edge the driveway, grass should be flush with the top of the curb so that no shaggy bits of grass remain after mowing.

The space beside the walls of the house can be handled in several ways. Some recommend a strip of paving against the foundation for easy access to exterior walls and windows. This is very popular in the West. One-story houses with a wide overhang and no eaves troughs may have a gravel or cobblestone gutter, 12 inches to 18 inches wide and 6 inches deep, centered under the drip line to pick up water from the roof. A brick or metal curb will help to contain the gravel; the top of this curb should be flush with the lawn. In some cases the entire area under the eaves is put into gravel or paved with cobblestones. Any planting should be placed outside the gravel gutter where it will not be injured by the drip.

A bed of ground cover, small shrubs or evergreens may be planted between the house wall and the gravel gutter; however, in many cases this bed will be dry and will need extra watering. This can easily be solved by installing a permanent section of perforated plastic pipe along the center line of the planting bed and connected to a hose bibb to supply water as needed. An automatic watering device for plant beds under the eaves can be made with a section of square or rectangular down-spout, fastened horizontally to the house foundation an inch or so below the base of the siding. These sections should have $3/16$-inch holes drilled at 6-inch intervals along the outer face. They are soldered into the vertical downspouts and when it rains the plant beds are adequately watered.

Planting beds around the house are often bordered by lawn. This is another place where a mowing strip should be used as a labor-saving device. Mowing strips can be made of concrete, brick, rectangular pieces of bluestone or solid concrete block 4 inches thick. A mowing strip 2 inches wide will allow the tip of a rotary blade to overlap. The wheel of a small reel mower will run along a mowing strip 4 inches wide, but riding mowers need a strip 6 to 8 inches across for best results.

Bricks are the easiest to use and the most attractive. Simply stake out a long gently flowing line using the rules for curves in Chapter 12. Use a mason's cord and 8-inch wooden plant labels or stout wire stakes, closely spaced. Adjust until the line flows attractively. In well-drained areas, just cut out the soil in a neat trench and install 4 by 8-inch brick, face up. The top of the brick should be level with the soil, or a bit above it in a new lawn. If the soil is not well-drained it may be necessary to use a 2-inch drainage base of sand or gravel beneath the brick. A landscape curb of metal, plastic or fiberglass may be installed along the lawn side of the curb to keep bricks in place and prevent grass roots from growing into their joints. This can also be prevented by using a strip of 6 mm. polyethylene plastic (available at building supply places) under and against the lawn face of the brick. Such a mowing strip is useful wherever lawn abuts ground cover beds, flower beds or shrub beds. It holds the line and permanently separates lawn from planted beds. While any mowing strip will be apparent when newly installed, it will become less visible as plants spread and moss covers the surface.

A mowing strip should also be used around trees on the lawn. Here a neat circle is made, using brick laid side by side. Keep the inside of the curb at least a foot from the trunk; large trees should have the mowing strip well beyond the butt swell. Inside the circle remove the soil and add a layer of washed gravel or bark mulch. A sheet of 6 mil polyethylene plastic under the mulch or gravel will prevent grass and weeds from growing. This mulch circle is effective even without the brick border. Mowing strips around trees have one great advantage: they remove any excuse for injuring tree trunks with the lawn mower.

Such obstructions as lamp posts, flagpoles, birdhouses and feeders on posts, oil-fill and vent pipes, and clothes-line poles are best surrounded by square or rectangular pieces of flagstone, with the top flush with the soil. A polyethylene sheet should go underneath and the pieces fitted together with the top flush with or slightly above the soil. Where the lawn borders a wall or solid fence, a mowing strip should keep grass far enough from the wall to allow the mower to make a clean sweep. A masonry wall may have a built-in mowing strip of concrete or a band of brick 8 inches wide; loose material such as gravel or crushed stone can be used if held in place by some kind of curb. Here too a polyethylene sheet under the stone will keep out grass and weeds.

Grass can be untidy and annoying when it grows under fences,

269. *A charming house with an apple tree-shaded terrace originally looked out on a square lawn bordered on each side by wide flower borders with a background of fencing. To reduce the amount of cultivated space and give the area a more interesting form, a circular grass panel was introduced to replace the original square and evergreens added for year-round effect. At the rear of the lawn a broad flight of steps leads to a swimming pool and terrace at a higher level.*

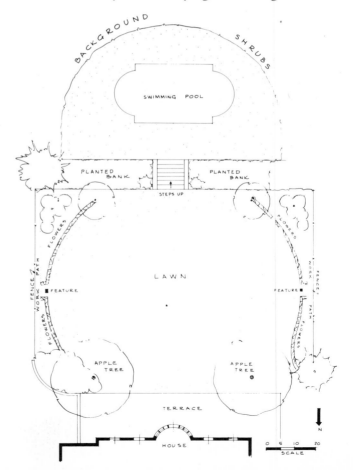

out of reach of the mower. Mowing strips can be used here too, providing they are wide enough for the mower to overlap them on each side of the fence. A post-and-rail fence may have the bottom rail high enough for the mower to reach underneath; circles of crushed stone enclosed by metal or plastic curbing can be installed around the posts to eliminate hand trimming.

It is important to allow space for the movement of wheeled equipment. If there is a sizeable change of grade involved, provide ramps of grass, paving or wood. As a safety measure it is wise to provide passage around the house, on one side at least, for fire and other emergency equipment.

If there is no lawn sprinkler system, provide hose bibbs or faucets

270. *To eliminate a large lawn to mow, the back area of this yard was planted with ground cover, keeping a grass walk leading to the vegetable garden.*

at convenient locations. Fifty feet of hose should reach all spots. Electric outlets should be included so that 50 feet of electric cord will service power tools, barbecues and outdoor lighting as needed. This is important if trimmed hedges are a part of the screen. Hedges that require no pruning require more space, but fences and screens of natural cedar allowed to weather require no care and take up little space.

And so we come to the end. It is hoped that through word and photo and drawing we have been able to convey some of the things that make for a workable, attractive and satisfying home landscape. As population pressures increase and more and more good land is covered with interstate highways and mammoth shopping centers, it behooves all of us to regard each precious square foot of the good earth as something to use wisely and conserve vigorously.

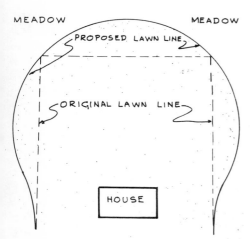

271. *If there is little change of grade simply carve out an easy flowing curved boundary for the mowed lawn shown as a solid line in plan. This is easier to live with and more easily mowed than the usual straight boundaries and square corners indicated as a dash line.*

272. *Any grass area that is constantly worn thin by traffic patterns should be replaced by some kind of paved walk or stepping-stones.*

273. *A metal mowing strip along a driveway, walk or path eliminates the tedious task of trimming and gives a neat, tidy appearance.*

GRASS   TERRACE

274. *Whenever possible, all paved areas should be flush or not more than an inch above the adjoining lawn.*

HOUSE   MOWED LAWN   SLOPE

MEADOW

275. *The transition between mowed lawn and meadow is nicely handled.*

HOUSE   MOWED LAWN   RETAINING WALL

MEADOW

276 (left). *A low retaining wall, separating lawn from meadow. The top of the wall should be flush with the lawn so the mower can overlap it.*

277 (left). *Mowing strips of concrete or flagstone at the base of a wall or building should be 8 inches wide.*

BUILDING OR WALL

FLAGSTONE OR CONCRETE MOWING STRIP 8" WIDE

LAWN

GRAVEL

SECTION

DRIP   HOUSE

LAWN

GRAVEL

PERFORATED PLASTIC PIPE

SECTION

278 and 279 (above and right). *If there are no eaves troughs to carry away the roof water, a gravel gutter along the house foundation is helpful as a drip line.*

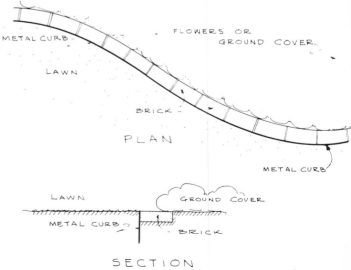

METAL CURB

FLOWERS OR GROUND COVER

LAWN

BRICK

PLAN

METAL CURB

280. *A brick mowing strip is an easy and attractive way to separate lawn from all kinds of planting beds. Bricks are laid end to end, flush with the soil or a bit above it. A curb of wood, metal or plastic between grass and brick will keep grass out of the joints.*

LAWN   GROUND COVER

METAL CURB   BRICK

SECTION

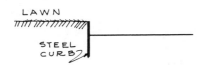
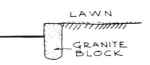

LAWN

STEEL CURB

DRIVEWAY

LAWN

GRANITE BLOCK

SECTION

281 (above). *If driveways have raised curbs of heavy steel or granite block, raise the lawn to be level with the top of the curb.*

282. *A brick mowing strip is one of several labor-saving devices for grass.*

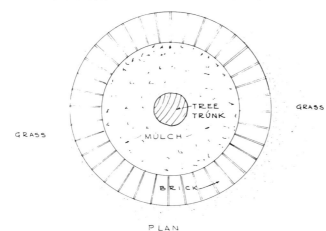

GRASS

TREE TRUNK

GRASS

MULCH

BRICK

PLAN

283 (left). *Protect trees in the lawn from mower injury and eliminate edging by using a circle of brick well away from the trunk.*

277

284. *A grass ramp is a simple way to maintain a gradual incline. The non-traffic area is put into ground cover.*

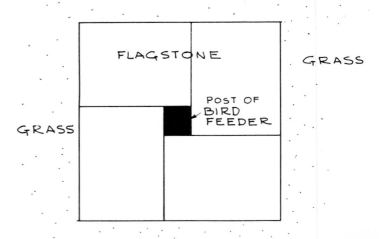

285 (right). *Use flush paving of flagstone around obstructions in the lawn.*

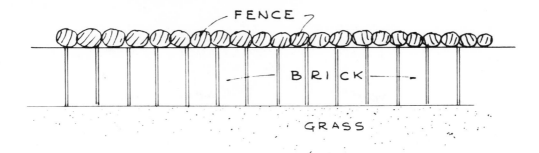

FENCE

BRICK

GRASS

286. Bricks laid side by side make a neat edge at the base of a fence.

287 (right). Eliminate hard-to-reach grass around base of fence posts.

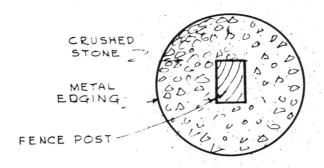

CRUSHED STONE

METAL EDGING

FENCE POST

288. A lawn sprinkler system is a wonderful asset and a real luxury, but if there is none, hose faucets at convenient locations make life a lot easier.

289. *A driveway border of evergreen shrubs needs only occasional pruning. The cemented Belgian block edging keeps the snowplow from destroying the beds.*

290. *A naturalistic (informal) entrance on a grade makes good use of a ground cover.*

291. *A pachysandra ground cover around a driveway with a metal lining strip is hard to beat for low maintenance.*

292. *A charming paved brick entrance with Vinca beds around the front of the house and a metal strip edging the driveway requires almost no maintenance.*

INDEX

INDEX

In a few cases, the authors have used landscape designs or photographs by other people. They are acknowledged here.